JACK P. GREENE

THE AMERICAN COLONIES
IN THE
EIGHTEENTH CENTURY
1689-1763

GOLDENTREE BIBLIOGRAPHIES

In American History

under the series editorship of

Arthur S. Link

Robert H. Bremner: AMERICAN SOCIAL HISTORY SINCE 1860

Robert E. Burke: THE TWENTIES AND THE NEW DEAL, 1920–1940

Nelson R. Burr: AMERICAN RELIGIOUS LIFE

E. David Cronon: THE SECOND WORLD WAR AND THE ATOMIC AGE, 1940–1968

Vincent P. De Santis: THE GILDED AGE, 1877–1896

David Donald: THE NATION IN CRISIS, 1861–1877

Don E. Fehrenbacher: MANIFEST DESTINY AND THE COMING OF THE CIVIL WAR, 1841–1860

E. James Ferguson: THE CONFEDERATION AND THE CONSTITUTION, 1781–1801

John Hope Franklin: AMERICAN NEGRO HISTORY

Paul M. Gaston: THE NEW SOUTH

Norman A. Graebner: AMERICAN DIPLOMATIC HISTORY BEFORE 1890

Fletcher M. Green: THE OLD SOUTH

(continued on inside back cover)

The American Colonies
in the Eighteenth Century
1689–1763

GOLDENTREE BIBLIOGRAPHIES

In American History

under the series editorship of

Arthur S. Link

The American Colonies
in the Eighteenth Century
1689–1763

compiled by

Jack P. Greene

The Johns Hopkins University

with the assistance of

Edward C. Papenfuse, Jr.

APPLETON-CENTURY CROFTS

Educational Division

New York   MEREDITH CORPORATION

Copyright © 1969 by

MEREDITH CORPORATION

All rights reserved

619–1

Library of Congress Card Number: 73-79166

PRINTED IN THE UNITED STATES OF AMERICA

390-38375-9

Editor's Foreword

GOLDENTREE BIBLIOGRAPHIES IN AMERICAN HISTORY are designed to provide students, teachers, and librarians with ready and reliable guides to the literature of American History in all its remarkable scope and variety. Volumes in the series cover comprehensively the major periods in American history, while additional volumes are devoted to all important subjects.

Goldentree Bibliographies attempt to steer a middle course between the brief list of references provided in the average textbook and the long bibliography in which significant items are often lost in the sheer number of titles listed. Each bibliography is, therefore, selective, with the sole criterion for choice being the significance—and not the age—of any particular work. The result is bibliographies of all works, including journal articles and doctoral dissertations, that are still useful, without bias in favor of any particular historiographical school.

Each compiler is a scholar long associated, both in research and teaching, with the period or subject of his volume. All compilers have not only striven to accomplish the objective of this series but have also cheerfully adhered to a general style and format. However, each compiler has been free to define his field, make his own selections, and work out internal organization as the unique demands of his period or subject have seemed to dictate.

The single great objective of *Goldentree Bibliographies in American History* will have been achieved if these volumes help researchers and students to find their way to the significant literature of American history.

Arthur S. Link

Compiler's Note

BUILDING ON AN earlier collection effort by Judith Hope Reynolds, Edward C. Papenfuse, Jr., collected the bibliographical data on the approximately 8,000 titles, from which the 2,000 entries here included were selected, and along with Sallie Papenfuse, typed the final manuscript. Edward M. Cook, Jr., Patricia A. Molen, and Alan Tully generously helped with the proofreading. I supplied the organizational framework and selected and arranged the entries. This bibliography does not list dissertations or collections of primary materials.

J. P. G.

Abbreviations

Ag Hist	Agricultural History
A L A Bull	A.L.A. Bulletin. Title varies.
Ala Rev	The Alabama Review: A Quarterly Journal of Alabama History
Am	Americana. Title varies.
Am Anthro	American Anthropologist
Am Archiv	American Archivist
Am Bar Assn J	American Bar Association Journal
Am Geneal	American Genealogist. Title varies.
Am Her	American Heritage
Am Hist Assn Ann Rep	American Historical Association Annual Report
Am Hist Rev	American Historical Review
Am J Dis Child	American Journal of Diseases of Children. Title varies.
Am J Leg Hist	American Journal of Legal History
Am J Socio	American Journal of Sociology
Am Jew Hist Soc Pub	American Jewish Historical Society Publications
Am Lit	American Literature; A Journal of Literary History, Criticism and Bibliography
Am Neptune	American Neptune; A Quarterly Journal of Maritime History
Am Ox	American Oxonian (Alumni Association of American Rhodes Scholars)
Am Pol Sci Rev	American Political Science Review
Am Q	American Quarterly
Am Socio Rev	American Sociological Review
Am Sp	American Speech
Ang Theol Rev	Anglican Theological Review
Ann Am Acad Pol Sci	Annals, American Academy of Political and Social Sciences, Philadelphia
Ann Assn Am Geog	Annals, Association of American Geographers
Ann Med Hist	Annals of Medical History
Ann Rep Smith Inst	Annual Report, Smithsonian Institution
Antiques	
Art Q	The Art Quarterly
Bar Mus Hist Soc J	Barbados Museum and Historical Society Journal
Berm Hist Q	Bermuda Historical Quarterly
Book at Brown	Friends of the Library of Brown University Books at Brown
Bos Pub Lib Q	Boston Public Library Quarterly
Bos U Law Rev	Boston University Law Review

Bull Conn Hist Soc	*Bulletin, Connecticut Historical Society*
Bull Frnds Hist Assn	*Bulletin, Friends' Historical Association, Philadelphia*
Bull Hist Med	*Bulletin of the History of Medicine.* Title varies.
Bull Inst Hist Res	*Bulletin of the Institute of Historical Research*
Bull N Y Acad Med	*Bulletin, New York Academy of Medicine*
Bull N Y Pub Lib	*Bulletin, New York Public Library*
Bus Hist Rev	*Business History Review.* Title varies.
Canad Bar Rev	*Canadian Bar Review*
Canad Hist Assn Rep	*Canadian Historical Association Reports.* Title varies.
Canad Hist Rev	*Canadian Historical Review*
Carib Q	*Caribbean Quarterly*
Carib Stud	*Caribbean Studies*
Cath Hist Rev	*Catholic Historical Review*
Ch Hist	*Church History*
Chymia	*Chymia: Annual Studies in the History of Chemistry*
Ciba	*Ciba Symposia*
Cithara	*Cithara: Essays in the Judeo-Christian Tradition*
Coll Am Statis Assn	*Collections, American Statistical Association*
Coll Mass Hist Soc	*Collections, Massachusetts Historical Society*
Commentary	*Commentary: A Jewish Review*
Comp Stud Hist Soc	*Comparative Studies in History and Society*
Conn Med J	*Connecticut Medicine.* Title varies.
Cornell Law Q	*Cornell Law Quarterly*
Dakota Law Rev	*Dakota Law Review*
Dal Rev	*Dalhousie Review*
Del Hist	*Delaware History*
Del Note	*Delaware Notes*
E Tenn Hist Soc Pub	*East Tennessee Historical Publications*
Econ Hist	*Economic History*
Econ Hist Rev	*Economic History Review*
E L H	*E L H; A Journal of English Literary History*
Eng Hist Rev	*English Historical Review*
Essex Inst Hist Coll	*Essex Institute Historical Collections*
Ethnohist	*Ethnohistory*
Etude	*Etude, The Music Magazine*
Explor Entrep Hist	*Explorations in Entrepreneurial History*
Franklin Inst J	*Franklin Institute Journal*
Fr Rev	*French Review*
Fr Stud	*French Studies: A Quarterly Review*
Ga Bar J	*Georgia Bar Journal*
Ga Hist Q	*Georgia Historical Quarterly*
Ga Rev	*Georgia Review*
Galleon	*The Galleon: Bulletin of the Society for Colonial History*
Geog Rev	*Geographical Review*
Har Alum Bull	*Harvard Alumni Bulletin*
Har Lib Bull	*Harvard Library Bulletin*

Har Theol Rev	*Harvard Theological Review*
His-Am Hist Rev	*Hispanic-American Historical Review*
Hist J	*Historical Journal.* Title varies.
Hist Mag P E Ch	*Historical Magazine of the Protestant Episcopal Church*
Hist Stud (Austral)	*Historical Studies, Australia and New Zealand*
Hist Theory	*History and Theory*
Hist Today	*History Today*
Historian	*The Historian: A Journal of History*
History	
Hop U Stud	*Johns Hopkins University Studies in Historical and Political Science*
Hunt Lib Bull	*Huntington Library Bulletin*
Hunt Lib Q	*The Huntington Library Quarterly: A Journal for the History and Interpretation of English Civilization*
Int Rec Med	*International Record of Medicine.* Title varies.
Isis	
J Am Hist	*Journal of American History*
J Am Phar	*Journal, American Pharmaceutical Association Practical Pharmacy Edition*
Jam Hist Rev	*Jamaican Historical Review*
James Sprunt Hist Stud	*James Sprunt Historical Studies.* Title varies.
J Brit Stud	*The Journal of British Studies*
J Chem Educ	*Journal of Chemical Education*
J Comp Legis	*Journal of Comparative Legislation and International Law*
J Crim Law	*Journal of Criminal Law, Criminology, and Police Science*
J Econ Bus Hist	*Journal of Economic and Business History*
J Econ Hist	*Journal of Economic History*
J Eng Ger Philol	*Journal of English and Germanic Philology.* Title varies.
J Hist Ideas	*Journal of the History of Ideas*
J Hist Med	*Journal of the History of Medicine and Allied Sciences*
J Med Assn Ga	*Journal, Medical Association of Georgia*
J Med Ed	*The Journal of Medical Education*
J Mod Hist	*Journal of Modern History*
J Neg Hist	*The Journal of Negro History*
J Ped	*Journal of Pediatrics*
J Pol Econ	*Journal of Political Economy*
J Presby Hist Soc	*Journal, Presbyterian Historical Society*
J Rel	*Journal of Religion*
J Rel Hist	*Journal of Religious History*
J Roy Artil	*Journal of the Royal Artillery*
J S Hist	*The Journal of Southern History*
J Soc Arch Hist	*Journal, Society of Architectural Historians*
J Soc Hist	*Journal of Social History*

J Trop Geog	*Journal of Tropical Geography*
Jew Q Rev	*Jewish Quarterly Review*
Lib Q	*Library Quarterly, A Journal of Investigation and Discussion in the Field of Library Science*
Mag Hist	*Magazine of History, with Notes and Queries*
Md Hist Mag	*Maryland Historical Review*
Menn Q Rev	*The Mennonite Quarterly Review*
Mich Hist Soc Coll	*Michigan Pioneer and Historical Society, Collections.* Title varies.
Mid-Am	*Mid-America*
Mil Affairs	*Military Affairs*
Minn Hist	*Minnesota History*
Miss Val Hist Rev	*Mississippi Valley Historical Review: A Journal of American History;* continued as *The Journal of American History*
Mod Lang Q	*Modern Language Quarterly*
Monat	*Monatshefte: A Journal Devoted to the Study of German Language and Literature.* Title varies.
More Book	(Predecessor of *Bos Pub Lib Q*)
Mus Q	*Musical Quarterly*
Muzzle Blasts	
N C Hist Rev	*North Carolina Historical Review*
N C Med J	*North Carolina Medical Journal*
N Eng Hist Geneal Reg	*New England Historical and Genealogical Register*
N Eng Mag	*New England Magazine.* Title varies.
N Eng Q	*New England Quarterly: An Historical Review of the New England Life and Letters*
N Eng Soc Stud Bull	*New England Social Studies Bulletin*
N Y Fklr Q	*New York Folklore Quarterly*
N Y Hist	*New York History* (New York State Historical Association)
N-Y Hist Soc Coll	*New-York Historical Society Collections*
N-Y Hist Soc Q	*New-York Historical Society Quarterly Bulletin*
N Y J Med	*New York State Journal of Medicine*
N Y Law Forum	*New York Law Forum*
N Y Law Rev	*New York Law Review*
N Y St Hist Assn J	*New York State Historical Association Quarterly Journal;* became *New York History*
N Y U Law Q Rev	*New York University Law Quarterly Review*
Nat Mag	*National Magazine*
Nat Rev	*National Review*
Note Rec Roy Soc London	*Notes and Records Royal Society of London*
Notes	
Numis	*Numismatist*
Old-Time N Eng	*Old-Time New England*
Pa-Ger	*The Pennsylvania-German.* Title varies.
Pa Ger Folk Soc Yr Bk	*Pennsylvania German Folklore Society Year Book*

Pa Hist	*Pennsylvania History*
Pa Mag Hist	*Pennsylvania Magazine of History and Biography*
Pap Am Soc Ch Hist	*Papers, American Society of Church History*
Pap Bibliog Soc Am	*Papers, Bibliographical Society of America*
Pap Lanc Co Hist Soc	*Historical Papers, Lancaster County (Pa) Historical Society*
Pap Mich Acad	*Papers, Michigan Academy of Science, Arts and Letters*
Pap N Haven Col Hist Soc	*Papers, New Haven Colony Historical Society*
Past Pres	*Past and Present; Studies in the History of Civilization*
Pers Am Hist	*Perspectives in American History*
Person	*Personalist: An International Review of Philosophy, Religion, and Literature*
Phila Geog Soc Bull	*Philadelphia Geographical Society Bulletin*
Pol Sci Q	*Political Science Quarterly*
Pol Stud	*Political Studies*
Princ Theo Rev	*Princeton Theological Review*
Proc Am Ant Soc	*Proceedings, American Antiquarian Society*
Proc Am Philos Soc	*Proceedings of the American Philosophical Society*
Proc Bos Soc	*Proceedings, Bostonian Society*
Proc Brit Acad	*Proceedings, British Academy for the Promotion of Historical, Philosophical and Philological Studies*
Proc Mass Hist Soc	*Proceedings, Massachusetts Historical Society*
Proc N J Hist Soc	*Proceedings, New Jersey Historical Society*
Proc N Y St Hist Assn	*Proceedings, New York State Historical Association*
Proc Pa-Ger Soc	*Proceedings and Addresses, Pennsylvania-German Society*
Proc Roy Geog Soc (Austral)	*Proceedings, Royal Geographical Society of Australia: South Australian Branch, . . .*
Proc Royal Soc Canad	*Proceedings, Royal Society of Canada*
Proc S C Hist Assn	*Proceedings, South Carolina Historical Association*
Proc Wis Hist Soc	*Proceedings, Wisconsin State Historical Society*
Pub Am Stat Assn	*Publications, American Statistical Association*
Pub Col Soc Mass	*Publications, Colonial Society of Massachusetts*
Pub Roch Hist Soc	*Publication Fund Series, Rochester Historical Society*
Q J Sp	*Quarterly Journal of Speech*
Q Rev Evan Luth Ch	*Quarterly Review of the Evangelical Lutheran Church.* Title varies.
R I Hist	*Rhode Island History*
R I Hist Soc Coll	*Rhode Island Historical Society, Collections*
R I Jew Hist Note	*Rhode Island Jewish Historical Notes*
Rec Am Cath Hist Soc	*Records, American Catholic Historical Society of Philadelphia*
Ren Mod Stud	*Renaissance and Modern Studies*
Rev Hist Am	*Revista de Historia de America*
Rev Hist Am Fr	*Revue d'histoire de l'Amerique Francaise*

Rev Pol	*The Review of Politics*
Rice Inst Pam	*Rice Institute Pamphlets*
Roy Hist Soc Trans	*Royal Historical Society, Transactions*
Roy Soc Canad Trans	*Royal Society of Canada, Transactions*
S Atl Q	*South Atlantic Quarterly*
S C Hist Assn Proc	*South Carolina Historical Association, Proceedings*
S C Hist Mag	*South Carolina Historical Magazine.* Title varies.
S Econ J	*The Southern Economic Journal*
S Ind Stud	*Southern Indian Studies*
S Q	*Southern Quarterly*
School Rev	*The School Review: A Journal of Secondary Education*
Sci Mo	*Scientific Monthly*
Sew Rev	*Sewanee Review*
Soc Forces	*Social Forces: A Scientific Medium of Social Study and Interpretation*
Soc Hist Ger Md	*Society for the History of the Germans in Maryland*
Soc Ser Rev	*The Social Service Review: A Quarterly Devoted to the Scientific and Professional Interests of Social Work*
Stud	*Studies; An Irish Quarterly Review of Letters, Philosophy, and Science*
Stud Philol	*Studies in Philology*
Temple Law Q	*Temple Law Quarterly.* Title varies.
Tenn Hist Q	*Tennessee Historical Quarterly*
Tex Rev	*Texas Review*
Theo Today	*Theology Today*
Thought	*Thought: A Quarterly of Sciences and Letters.* Title varies.
Trans Wis Acad Sci	*Transactions, Wisconsin Academy of Sciences, Arts and Letters*
U Birmingham Hist J	*University of Birmingham Historical Journal*
U Colo Stud	*University of Colorado Studies.* Title varies.
U Pa Law Rev	*University of Pennsylvania Law Review and American Law Register*
U S Cath Hist Rec	*U.S. Catholic Historical Society, Historical Records and Studies*
U S N Inst Proc	*U.S. Naval Institute Proceedings*
Va Law Rev	*Virginia Law Review*
Va Mag Hist	*Virginia Magazine of History and Biography*
W Pa Hist Mag	*Western Pennsylvania Historical Magazine*
W Va Hist	*West Virginia History, A Quarterly Magazine*
W Va Law Q	*West Virginia Law Quarterly and the Bar.* Title varies.
Wm Mar Q	*William and Mary Quarterly*
Wor Pol	*World Politics*
Yale J Biol Med	*Yale Journal of Biology and Medicine*
Yale Law J	*Yale Law Journal*

Yale Rev	*Yale Review*
Yale U Lib Gaz	*Yale University Library Gazette*
Yr Bk Charleston S C	*Year Book, Charleston, South Carolina*

Note: Cross-references are to page (**Boldface**) and to item numbers (roman). Items marked by a dagger (†) are available in paperback edition at the time this bibliography goes to press. The publisher and compiler invite suggestions for additions to future editions of the bibliography.

Contents

CONTENTS

Bibliographies

Other bibliographies of specialized materials are listed below in the relevant sections.

1 BEERS, Henry P. *Bibliographies in American History; Guide to Materials for Research.* New York, 1942.

2 BELLOT, H. Hale. "The Mainland Colonies in the Eighteenth Century." *History,* XVII (1933), 344-350.

3 BILLINGTON, Ray A., ed. *The Reinterpretation of Early American History: Essays in Honor of John Edwin Pomfret.* San Marino, Calif., 1966.†

4 BRIGHAM, Clarence. *History and Bibliography of American Newspapers, 1690-1820.* 2 vols. Worcester, Mass., 1947.

5 CLARK, Thomas D. *Travels in the Old South: A Bibliography.* 2 vols. Norman, Okla., 1956.

6 DAVIES, Godfrey. *Bibliography of British History, Stuart Period, 1603-1714.* Oxford, 1928.

7 EVANS, Charles. *The American Bibliography of Charles Evans.* 14 vols. Worcester, Mass., 1959.

8 FURBER, Elizabeth C., ed. *Changing Views on British History; Essays on Historical Writing since 1939.* Cambridge, Mass., 1966.

9 GREENE, Jack P. "The Publication of the Official Records of the Southern Colonies." *Wm Mar Q,* 3rd ser., XIV (1957), 268-280.

10 GROSE, Clyde L. *A Select Bibliography of British History, 1660-1760.* Chicago, 1939.

11 HANDLIN, Oscar, and others. *Harvard Guide to American History.* New York, 1967.†

12 HARPER, Lawrence A. "Recent Contributions to American Economic History. American History to 1789." *J Econ Hist,* XIX (1959), 1-24.

13 LARNED, J. N., ed. *The Literature of American History, A Bibliographical Guide, , , ,* Boston, 1902.

14 MATTHEWS, William. *American Diaries: An Annotated Bibliography of American Diaries Written Prior to the Year 1861."* Berkeley, Calif., 1945.

15 MERENESS, Newton D., ed. *Travels in the American Colonies.* New York, 1916.

16 MIDDLEKAUF, Robert L. "The American Continental Colonies in the Empire." In *Historiography of the British Empire-Commonwealth.* Ed. Robin W. Winks. Durham, N.C., 1966.

17 MILNE, Alexander T. *Writings on British History (1934-1945). . . .* London, 1937-1960.

18 MORGAN, William T. *A Bibliography of British History (1700-1715) with Special Reference to the Reign of Queen Anne.* 5 vols. Bloomington, Ind., 1934-1942.

19 PARGELLIS, Stanley and D. J. MEDLEY, eds. *Bibliography of British History. The Eighteenth Century, 1714-1789.* Oxford, 1951.

1 PRAGER, Herta and William W. PRICE. "A Bibliography on the History of the Courts of the Thirteen Original Colonies, Maine, Ohio, and Vermont." *Am J Leg Hist*, I (1957), 336-362; II (1958), 35-52, 148-154.

2 ROOS, Frank J. *Writings on Early American Architecture: An Annotated List....* Columbus, Ohio, 1943.

3 RULE, John C. "The Old Regime in America: A Review of Recent Interpretations of France in America." *Wm Mar Q,* 3rd ser., XIX (1962), 575-600.

4 SABIN, Joseph A. *Bibliotheca Americana. A Dictionary of Books Relating to America from its Discovery to the Present Time.* 29 vols. New York, 1868-1936.

5 WEED, Katherine K. and Richmond P. BOND. *Studies of British Newspapers and Periodicals from their Beginning to 1800. Stud Philol,* Ex. Ser. No.2 (1946).

6 WINSOR, Justin, ed. *Narrative and Critical History of America.* 8 vols. Boston, 1884-1889.

7 *Writings on American History, 1902-*   Princeton, New York, New Haven, and Washington, D.C., 1904-

The International Scene

The following list is highly selective. For further reading consult the extensive bibliographies below under the heading *General*.

General

8 DORN, Walter L. *Competition for Empire, 1740-1763.* New York, 1940.†

9 *The New Cambridge Modern History.* Ed. J. O. Lindsay. Vol. V, *The Ascendancy of France.* Cambridge, Eng., 1961. Vol. VII, *The Old Regime ,* *1713-1763.* Cambridge, Eng., 1957.

10 ROBERTS, Penfield. *The Quest for Security, 1715-1740.* New York, 1947.†

11 WOLF, John B. *The Emergence of the Great Powers, 1685-1715.* New York, 1951.†

The Intellectual Context

12 BECKER, Carl L. *The Heavenly City of the Eighteenth-Century Philosophers.* New Haven, 1932.†

13 GAY, Peter. *The Enlightenment: An Interpretation. The Rise of Modern Paganism.* New York, 1966.

14 GAY, Peter. *The Party of Humanity: Essays in the French Enlightenment.* New York, 1964.

1 HAZARD, Paul. *European Thought in the Eighteenth Century from Montesquieu to Lessing.* London 1954.†

2 LOVEJOY, Arthur O. *The Great Chain of Being: A Study of the History of an Idea.* London, 1936.†

3 LOVEJOY, Arthur O. *Reflections on Human Nature.* Baltimore, 1962.

4 MANUEL, Frank E. *The Age of Reason.* Ithaca, 1951.†

5 MARTIN, Kingsley. *French Liberal Thought in the Eighteenth Century.* New York, 1963.†

The British Background

The following brief list is necessarily highly selective. For further listings see the extensive bibliographies in 1:19.

General

6 CLARK, Sir George. *The Later Stuarts, 1660-1714.* 2nd ed. Oxford, 1961.

7 HILL, Christopher. *The Century of Revolution, 1603-1714.* Edinburgh, 1961.†

8 MALCOLM-SMITH, Elizabeth F. *British Diplomacy in the Eighteenth Century, 1700-1789.* London, 1937.

9 MARSHALL, Dorothy. *Eighteenth Century England.* London, 1962.

10 OGG, David. *England in the Reigns of James II and William III.* Oxford, 1957.

11 PLUMB, J. H. *The First Four Georges.* New York, 1957.

12 TREVELYAN, G. M. *England under Queen Anne.* 3 vols. London, 1931-1934.

13 WILLIAMS, Basil. *The Whig Supremacy, 1714-1760.* Oxford, 1939.

Biography

14 BAXTER, Stephen B. *William III and the Defense of European Liberty, 1650-1702.* New York, 1966.

15 CRANSTON, Maurice. *John Locke: A Biography.* London, 1957.

16 HART, Jeffrey. *Viscount Bolingbroke: Tory Humanist.* Toronto, 1965.

17 KENYON, John P. *Robert Spencer, Earl of Sunderland, 1641-1702.* London, 1958.

18 NULLE, Stebelton H. *Thomas Pelham-Hollis, Duke of Newcastle: His Early Political Career, 1693-1724.* Philadelphia, 1931.

19 PLUMB, J. H. *Sir Robert Walpole: The King's Minister.* London, 1960.

20 PLUMB, J. H. *Sir Robert Walpole: The Making of a Statesman.* London, 1956.

21 ROBERTSON, Charles G. *Chatham and the British Empire.* London, 1946.†

22 SHERRARD, Owen A. *Lord Chatham and America.* London, 1958.

1 SHERRARD, Owen A. *Lord Chatham: Pitt and the Seven Years' War.* London, 1955.

2 WILKES, John W. *A Whig in Power: The Political Career of Henry Pelham.* Evanston, Ill., 1964.

3 WILLIAMS, Basil. *Carteret and Newcastle.* Cambridge, Eng., 1943.

4 WILLIAMS, Basil. *The Life of William Pitt, Earl of Chatham.* 2 vols. London, 1913.

The Public World

THE INSTITUTIONAL AND CONSTITUTIONAL SETTING

5 BAXTER, Stephen B. *The Development of the Treasury, 1660-1702.* Cambridge, Mass., 1957.

6 BEER, Samuel H. "The Representation of Interests in British Government: Historical Background." *Am Pol Sci Rev,* LI (1957), 613-650.

7 EHRMAN, John. *The Navy in the War of William III, 1689-1697.* Cambridge, Mass., 1953.

8 ELLIS, Kenneth. *The Post Office in the Eighteenth Century: A Study in Administrative History.* London, 1958.

9 FOORD, Archibald S. *His Majesty's Opposition, 1714-1830.* Oxford, 1964.

10 HOON, Elizabeth E. *The Organization of the English Customs System, 1696-1786.* New York, 1938.

11 HORN, D. B. *The British Diplomatic Service, 1689-1789.* Oxford, 1961.

12 POOL, Bernard. *Navy Board Contracts, 1660-1832: Contract Administration under the Navy Board.* Hamden, Conn., 1966.

13 REITAN, E. A. "The Civil List in Eighteenth-Century British Politics: Parliamentary Supremacy Versus the Independence of the Crown." *Hist J,* IX (1966), 318-337.

14 ROBERTS, Clayton. *The Growth of Responsible Government in Stuart England.* Cambridge, Eng., 1966.

15 THOMSON, Mark A. *A Constitutional History of England, 1642 to 1801.* London, 1938.

16 THOMSON, Mark A. *The Secretaries of State, 1681-1782.* Oxford, 1932.

17 TURNER, Edward R. *The Privy Council of England in the Seventeenth and Eighteenth Centuries, 1603-1784.* 2 vols. Baltimore, 1927-1928.

18 WARD, William R. *The English Land Tax in the Eighteenth Century.* Oxford, 1953.

19 WESTON, Corinne C. *English Constitutional Theory and the House of Lords, 1556-1832.* New York, 1965.

20 WILLIAMS, E. Neville, ed. *The Eighteenth Century Constitution, 1688-1815, Documents and Commentary.* Cambridge, Eng., 1960.

THE STRUCTURE OF POLITICS

1 FEILING, Keith. *History of the Tory Party, 1640-1714.* Oxford, 1924.

2 FRYER, W. R. "The Study of British Politics between the Revolution and the Reform Act." *Ren Mod Stud,* I (1957), 91-114.

3 HENDERSON, Alfred J. *London and the National Government, 1721-1742.* Durham, N.C., 1945.

4 HOLMES, Geoffrey. *British Politics in the Age of Anne.* New York, 1967.

5 HORWITZ, Henry. "Parties, Connections, and Parliamentary Politics, 1689-1714: Review and Revision." *J Brit Stud,* VI (1966), 45-69.

6 JONES, George H. *The Main Stream of Jacobitism.* Cambridge, Mass., 1954

7 JUDD, Gerrit P., IV. *Members of Parliament, 1734-1832.* New Haven, 1955.

8 KEMP, Betty. *King and Commons, 1660-1832.* London, 1957.

9 KENYON, John P. *The Nobility in the Revolution of 1688.* Hull, Eng. 1963.

10 LAPRADE, William T. *Public Opinion and Politics in Eighteenth Century England to the Fall of Walpole.* New York, 1936.

11 NAMIER, Sir Lewis. *England in the Age of the American Revolution.* 2nd ed. London, 1961.†

12 NAMIER, Sir Lewis. *The Structure of British Politics at the Accession of George III.* 2nd ed. London, 1957.†

13 NAMIER, Sir Lewis and John BROOKE. *The History of Parliament: The House of Commons, 1754-1790.* 3 vols. New York, 1964.

14 OWEN, John B. *The Rise of the Pelhams.* London, 1957.

15 PENSON, Lillian M. "The London West India Interest in the Eighteenth Century." *Eng Hist Rev,* XXXVI (1921), 373-392.

16 PERRY, Thomas W. *Public Opinion, Propaganda, and Politics in Eighteenth Century England.* Cambridge, Mass., 1962.

17 PINKHAM, Lucile. *William III and the Respectable Revolution: The Part Played by William of Orange in the Revolution of 1688.* Cambridge, Mass., 1954.

18 PLUMB, J. H. *The Growth of Political Stability in England, 1675-1725.* London, 1967.

19 RUBINI, Dennis. *Court and Country 1688-1702.* London, 1967.

20 SUTHERLAND, Lucy M. "The City of London in Eighteenth-Century Politics." In *Essays Presented to Sir Lewis Namier,* Ed. Richard Pares and A. J. P. Taylor. London, 1956.

21 WALCOTT, Robert. *English Politics in the Early Eighteenth Century.* Cambridge, Mass., 1956.

22 WESTERN, J. R. *The English Militia in the Eighteenth Century: The Story of a Political Issue, 1660-1802.* Toronto, 1965.

1 WIGGIN, Lewis M. *The Faction of Cousins: A Political Account of the Grenvilles, 1733-1763.* New Haven, 1958.

POLITICAL CULTURE

2 BRIGGS, Asa. "The Language of 'Class' in Early Nineteenth Century England." *Essays in Labour History.* Ed. Asa Briggs and John Saville. New York, 1960, 43-73.

3 BURNS, J. H. "Bolingbroke and the Concept of Constitutional Government." *Pol Stud,* X (1962), 264-276.

4 CARPENTER, William S. "The Separation of Powers in the Eighteenth Century." *Am Pol Sci Rev,* XXII (1928), 32-44.

5 DOBREE, Bonamy. "The Theme of Patriotism in the Poetry of the Early Eighteenth Century." *Proc Brit Acad,* XXXV (1949), 49-65.

6 FINK, Zera S. *The Classical Republicans: An Essay in the Recovery of a Pattern of Thought in Seventeenth Century England.* Evanston, Ill., 1950.

7 GOUGH, John W. *John Locke's Political Philosophy: Eight Studies.* London, 1950.

8 GWYN, W. B. *The Meaning of the Separation of Powers.* New Orleans, 1965.

9 JACKMAN, Sydney W. *Man of Mercury: An Appreciation of the Mind of Henry St. John, Viscount Bolingbroke.* London, 1965.

10 KENDALL, Wilmoor. *John Locke and the Doctrine of Majority Rule.* Urbana, Ill., 1941.†

11 KRAMNICK, Isaac. *Bolingbroke and His Circle: The Politics of Nostalgia in the Age of Walpole.* Cambridge, Mass., 1968.

12 LASLETT, Peter, ed. *Patriarcha and Other Political Works of Sir Robert Filmer.* Oxford, 1949.

13 LOFTIS, John. *The Politics of Drama in Augustan England.* New York, 1963.

14 MC KILLOP, Alan D. *The Background of Thomson's Liberty. Rice Inst Pam,* XXXVIII (1951).

15 MACPHERSON, C. B. *The Political Theory of Possessive Individualism.* New York, 1962. †

16 MANSFIELD, Harvey E., Jr. *Statemanship and Party Government: A Study of Burke and Bolingbroke.* Chicago, 1965.

17 POCOCK, J. G. A. *The Ancient Constitution and the Feudal Law: English Historical Thought in the Seventeenth Century.* Cambridge, Eng., 1957. †

18 POCOCK, J. G. A. "Machiavelli, Harrington, and English Political Ideologies in the Eighteenth Century." *Wm Mar Q,* 3rd ser., XXII (1965), 547-583.

19 ROBBINS, Caroline. *The Eighteenth-Century Commonwealthman: Studies in the Transmission, Development, and Circumstance of English Liberal Thought from the Restoration of Charles II until the War with the Thirteen Colonies.* Cambridge, Mass., 1959.†

20 SHACKLETON, Robert. *Montesquieu.* Oxford, 1961.

1 SHACKLETON, Robert. "Montesquieu, Bolingbroke, and the Separation of Powers." *Fr Stud,* III (1949), 25-38.

2 SKINNER, Quentin. "History and Ideology in the English Revolution." *Hist J.* VIII (1965), 151-178.

3 STEWART, John B. *The Moral and Political Philosophy of David Hume.* New York, 1963.

4 VILE, M. J. C. *Constitutionalism and the Separation of Powers.* Oxford, 1967.

Economic and Social Development

GENERAL

5 ASHTON, T. S. *Economic Fluctuations in England, 1700-1800.* Oxford, 1959.

6 ASHTON, T. S. *An Economic History of England: The Eighteenth Century.* New York, 1955.

7 CLAPHAM, Sir John. *A Concise Economic History of Britain. From the Earliest Times to 1750.* Cambridge, Eng. 1963. †

8 DEANE, Phyllis and W. A. COLE. *British Economic Growth, 1688-1959: Trends and Structure.* New York, 1967.

9 EAST, W. G. "England in the Eighteenth Century." In *An Historical Geography of England before A. D. 1800; . . . ,* ed. H.C. Darby. Cambridge, Eng., 1936.

10 HABAKKUK, H. J. "The Economic History of Modern Britain." *J Econ Hist,* XVIII (1958), 486-501.

11 JOHN, A. H. "War and the English Economy, 1700-1763." *Econ Hist Rev,* VII (1955), 329-344.

12 LIPSON, Ephraim. *The Economic History of England.* 3 vols. London, 1931.

13 PRESSNELL, L.S., ed. *Studies in the Industrial Revolution Presented to T. S. Ashton.* London, 1960.

14 WILSON, Charles H. *Anglo-Dutch Commerce and Finance in the Eighteenth Century.* Cambridge, Eng., 1941.

15 WILSON, Charles H. *England's Apprenticeship, 1603-1763.* New York, 1965.

16 WRIGLEY, E. A. "A Simple Model of London's Importance in Changing English Society and Economy. 1650-1750." *Past Pres,* XXXVII (1967), 44-70.

DEMOGRAPHY

17 GLASS, D. W. and D. E. C. EVERSLEY, eds. *Population in History: Essays in Historical Demography.* Chicago, 1965.

18 WRIGLEY, E. A. *An Introduction to English Historical Demography from the Sixteenth to the Nineteenth Century.* New York, 1966.

LAND UTILIZATION

1 COLEMEN, D. C. "London Scriveners and the Estate Market in the Later Seventeenth Century." *Econ Hist Rev,* IV (1951), 221-230.

2 HABAKKUK, H. J. "English Land Market in the 18th Century." *Britain and the Netherlands.* Ed. J. S. Bromley and E.H. Kossmann. London, 1960.

3 HABBAKKUK, H. J. "English Landownership, 1680-1740." *Econ Hist Rev* 1st ser., X (1940), 2-17.

4 JOHN, A. H. "Agricultural Productivity and Economic Growth in England, 1700-1760." *J Econ Hist,* XXV (1965), 19-34.

5 JONES, E. L., ed. *Agriculture and Economic Growth in England 1650-1815.* London, 1967.

6 MINGAY, G.E. "The Agricultural Depression, 1730-1750." *Econ Hist Rev,* VIII (1956), 323-338.

7 MINGAY, G.E. *English Landed Society in the Eighteenth Century.* Toronto, 1963.

TRADE

8 ATTON, Henry and Henry H. HOLLAND. *The King's Customs, an Account of Maritime Revenue and Contraband Traffic in England, Scotland, and Ireland, from the Earliest Times to the Year 1800.* London, 1908.

9 BARKER, T. C. "Smuggling in the Eighteenth Century: The Evidence of the Scottish Tobacco Trade." *Va Mag Hist,* LXII (1954), 387-399.

10 CARSWELL, John. *The South Sea Bubble.* Palo Alto, 1960.

11 CLARK, George N. *Guide to English Commercial Statistics, 1696-1782.* London, 1938.

12 COLE, W. A. "Trends in Eighteenth-Century Smuggling." *Econ Hist Rev,* X (1958), 395-410.

13 DAVIES, K. G. *The Royal African Company.* London, 1957.

14 DAVIS, Ralph. *A Commercial Revolution: English Overseas Trade in the Seventeenth and Eighteenth Centuries.* London, 1967. †

15 DAVIS, Ralph. "English Foreign Trade, 1660-1700." *Econ Hist Rev,* VII (1954-1955), 150-166.

16 DAVIS, Ralph. "English Foreign Trade, 1700-1774." *Econ Hist Rev,* XV (1962-1963), 285-303.

17 DAVIS, Ralph. "Merchant Shipping in the Economy of the Late Seventeenth Century," *Econ Hist Rev,* IX (1956), 59-73.

18 DAVIS, Ralph. *The Rise of the English Shipping Industry in the Seventeenth and Eighteenth Centuries.* New York, 1962.

19 HINTON, Raymond W. K. *The Eastland Trade and the Common Weal in the Seventeenth Century.* Cambridge, Eng., 1959.

20 INNES, Arthur D. *The Maritime and Colonial Expansion of England under the Stuarts (1603-1714).* London, 1932.

21 INNIS, Harold A. *The Cod Fisheries: The History of an International Economy.* Oxford, 1940.

1 PLUMB, J.H. "The Mercantile Interest: The Rise of the British Merchant after 1689." *Hist Today*, V (1955), 762-767.

2 RAMSAY, G.D. *English Overseas Trade during the Centuries of Emergence: Studies in Some Modern Origins of the English-Speaking World*. London, 1957.

3 RICH, Edwin E. *Hudson's Bay Company, 1670-1870*. London, 1958.

4 SCHUMPETER, Elizabeth B. *English Overseas Trade Statistics, 1697-1808*. Oxford, 1960.

5 SPERLING, John G. *The South Sea Company: An Historical Essay and Bibliographical Finding List*. Boston, 1962.

6 WILLIAMS, Glyndwr. *The British Search for the Northwest Passage in the Eighteenth Century*. London, 1962.

BANKING

7 CLAPHAM, Sir John. *The Bank of England: A History, 1694-1914*. 2 vols. Cambridge, Eng., 1944.

8 DICKSON, Peter M. G. *The Financial Revolution in England, 1688-1756*. New York, 1967.

9 RICHARDS, Richard D. *Early History of Banking in England*. London, 1929.

10 VICKERS, Douglas. *Studies in the Theory of Money, 1690-1776*.

INDUSTRIALIZATION

11 COURT, William H. B. *The Rise of the Midland Industries, 1600-1828. Oxford, 1953*.

12 MANTOUX, Paul. *The Industrial Revolution in the Eighteenth Century; An Outline of the Beginnings of the Modern Factory System in England*. Rev. ed. London, 1928.†

13 PELHAM, R. A. "The West Midland Iron Industry and the American Market in the Eighteenth Century." *U Birmingham Hist J*, II (1950), 141-162.

SOCIAL STRUCTURE, VALUES, AND THE PROFESSIONS

14 BAHLMAN, Dudley W. R. *Moral Revolution of 1688*. New Haven, 1957.

15 GEORGE, Mary D., ed. *England in Johnson's Day*. London, 1928.

16 GEORGE, Mary D. *English Social Life in the Eighteenth Century* .... London, 1923.

17 GEORGE, Mary D. *London Life in the XVIIIth Century*. New York, 1925.†

18 HAMILTON, Bernice. "The Medical Profession in the Eighteenth Century." *Econ Hist Rev*, IV, (1951), 141-169.

19 HABAKKUK, H. J. "Marriage Settlements in the 18th Century." *Royal Hist Soc Trans*, XXXII (1950), 15-30.

20 HECHT, J. Jean. *Continental and Colonial Servants in Eighteenth Century England*. Northampton, Mass., 1954.

1 HECHT, J. Jean. *The Domestic Servant Class in Eighteenth-Century England.* London, 1956.

2 HUMPHREYS, A. R. *The Augustan World: Society, Thought, Letters in Eighteenth Century England.* London, 1954.†

3 LASLETT, Peter. *The World We Have Lost.* New York, 1965.

4 ROBSON, Robert. *The Attorney in Eighteenth Century England.* Cambridge, Eng., 1959.

5 SCHLATTER, Richard B. *Social Ideas of Religious Leaders, 1660-1668.* Oxford, 1940.

6 STONE, Lawrence. "Social Mobility in England, 1500-1700." *Past Pres,* XXXIII (1966), 16-55.

Culture

7 BATE, Walter J. *From Classic to Romantic: Premises of Taste in Eighteenth Century England.* Cambridge, Mass., 1946.†

8 BETHELL, Samuel. *The Cultural Revolution of the Seventeenth Century.* London, 1951.

9 BURTT, Edwin A. *The Metaphysics of Sir Isaac Newton: an Essay on the Metaphysical Foundations of Modern Science.* London, 1925.

10 BUTT, John E. *The Augustan Age.* London, 1950.†

11 DAVIS, Herbert. "The Augustan Conception of History," in *Reason and the Imagination: Studies in the History of Ideas, 1600-1800.* Ed. J. A. Mazzeo, New York, 1962.

12 DOBREE, Bonamy. *English Literature in the Early Eighteenth Century, 1700-1740.* Vol. VII, *The Oxford History of English Literature.* Oxford, 1959.

13 FLEMING, John. *Robert Adam and his Circle in Edinburgh and Rome.* Cambridge, Mass., 1962.

14 FUSSELL, Paul. *The Rhetorical World of Augustan Humanism: Ethics and Imagery from Swift to Burke.* Oxford, 1965.

15 HANS, Nicholas A. *New Trends in Education in the Eighteenth Century.* London, 1951.

16 KING, Lester S. *The Medical World of the Eighteenth Century.* Chicago, 1958.

17 PAULSON, Ronald. *Satire and the Novel in Eighteenth-Century England.* New Haven 1967.

18 SIEBERT, Frederick S. *Freedom of the Press in England, 1476-1776.* Urbana, Ill., 1952.†

19 SMITHERS, Peter. *Joseph Addison.* Oxford, 1954.

20 STEPHEN, Leslie. *History of English Thought in the Eighteenth Century.* 2 vols. New York, 1927.†

21 STROMBERG, R. I. "History in the Eighteenth Century," *J Hist Ideas,* XII (1951), 295-304.

22 SUMMERSON, John N. *Architecture in Britain, 1530-1830.* London, 1953.

23 SUMMERSON, John N. *Sir Christopher Wren.* London, 1953.

1 SYFRET, Rosemary H. "The Origins of the Royal Society." *Note Rec Roy Soc London,* V (1948), 75-137.

2 WARD, William R. *Georgian Oxford: University Politics in the Eighteenth Century.* Oxford, 1958.

3 WATERHOUSE, Ellis K. *Painting in Britain, 1530-1790.* London, 1953.

4 WESTFALL, Richard S. *Science and Religion in Seventeenth-Century England.* New Haven, 1958.

5 WHIFFEN, Marcus. *Stuart and Georgian Churches: The Architecture of the Church of England Outside London, 1603-1837.* London, 1948.

6 WHINNEY, Margaret D. and Oliver MILLER. *English Art, 1625-1714.* Vol. VIII, *The Oxford History of English Art.* Oxford, 1957.

7 WILLEY, Basil. *The Eighteenth-Century Background: Studies on the Idea of Nature in the Thought of the Period.* London, 1940.†

8 WILLEY, Basil. *The Seventeenth-Century Background: Studies in the Thought of the Age in Relation to Poetry and Religion.* London, 1935.†

Religion

9 COLIE, Rosalie L. *Light and Enlightenment: A Study of the Cambridge Platonists and the Dutch Arminians.* Cambridge, Eng., 1957.

10 CRAGG, Gerald R. *From Puritanism to the Age of Reason: A Study of Changes in Religious Thought within the Church of England, 1660 to 1700.* Cambridge, Eng., 1950.†

11 CRAGG, Gerald R. *Puritanism in the Period of the Great Persecution, 1660-1688.* Cambridge., Eng., 1957.

12 CRAGG, Gerald R. *Reason and Authority in the Eighteenth Century.* Cambridge, Eng., 1964.

13 DAVIES, Horton. *Worship and Theology in England: From Watts and Wesley to Maurice, 1690-1850.* Princeton, 1961.

14 LLOYD, Arnold. *Quaker Social History, 1669-1738.* London, 1950.

15 STROMBERG, Roland N. *Religious Liberalism in Eighteenth-Century England.* London, 1954.

16 SYKES, Norman. *Church and State in England in the Eighteenth Century.* Cambridge, Eng., 1934.

17 SYKES, Norman. *From Sheldon to Secker: Aspects of English Church History, 1660-1768.* New York, 1959.

18 SYKES, Norman. *William Wake, Archbishop of Canterbury, 1657-1737.* 2 vols. Cambridge, Eng., 1957.

Relations with the Colonies

GENERAL

19 ANDREWS, Charles M. *The Colonial Background of the American Revolution, Four Essays in American Colonial History.* Rev. ed. New Haven, 1931.†

1 KEITH, A. Berriedale. *Constitutional History of the First British Empire.* Oxford, 1930.

2 KNORR, Klaus E. *British Colonial Theories, 1570-1850.* Toronto, 1944.

3 KOEBNER, Richard. *Empire.* Cambridge, Eng., 1961.†

4 LABAREE, Leonard W., ed. *Royal Instructions to British Colonial Governors, 1670-1776.* New York, 1935.

5 REESE, Trevor. "Colonial America and Early New South Wales: Introductory Notes to a Comparative Survey of British Administrative Policies." *Hist Stud* (Austral), IX (1959), 74-84.

6 ROBERTSON, Sir Charles Grant. "The Imperial Problem in North America in the 18th Century (1714-1783)." *U Birmingham Hist J,* I (1947), 134-157.

7 WILSON, Charles. *England's Apprenticeship, 1603-1763.* See 7.15.

8 WILSON, Charles. "Mercantilism: Some Vicissitudes of an Idea." *Econ Hist Rev,* X (1957), 181-188.

INSTITUTIONAL FRAMEWORK

Crown and Privy Council

9 ANDREWS, Charles M. "The Royal Disallowance." *Proc Am Ant Soc,* XXIV (1914), 342-362.

10 DORLAND, Arthur G. *The Royal Disallowance in Massachusetts.* Kingston, Ont., 1917.

11 EGERTON, Hugh E. "The Seventeenth and Eighteenth Century Privy Council in its Relations with the Colonies." *J Comp Legis,* VII (1925), 1-16.

12 HAZELTINE, Harold D. "Appeals from Colonial Courts to the King in Council." *Am Hist Assn Ann Rep ,*(1894), 299-330.

13 RUSSELL, Elmer B. *The Review of American Colonial Legislation by the King in Council.* New York, 1915.

14 SCHLESINGER, Arthur M. "Colonial Appeals to the Privy Council." *Pol Sci Q,* XXVIII (1913), 279-297, 433-450.

15 SMITH, Joseph Henry. *Appeals to the Privy Council from the American Plantations.* New York, 1950.

16 WASHBURNE, George A. *Imperial Control of the Administration of Justice in the Thirteen American Colonies, 1684-1776.* New York, 1923.

The Board of Trade and Its Predecessor

17 BASYE, Arthur H. *The Lords Commissioners of Trade and Plantations, Commonly known as the Board of Trade, 1748-1782.* New Haven, 1925.

18 BIEBER, Ralph Paul. *The Lords of Trade and Plantations, 1675-1696.* Allentown, Pa., 1919.

19 CLARKE, Mary Patterson. "The Board of Trade at Work." *Am Hist Rev,* XVII (1911), 17-43.

20 DICKERSON, Oliver M. *American Colonial Government 1696-1765; A study of the British Board of Trade in its Relation to the American Colonies, Political, Industrial, Administrative.* Cleveland, 1912.

1 LASLETT, Peter. "John Locke, the Great Recoinage, and the Origins of the Board of Trade, 1695-1698." *Wm Mar Q*, 3d ser., XIV (1957), 370-402.

2 ROOT, Winfred T. "The Lords of Trade and Plantations, 1675-1696." *Am Hist Rev*, XXIII (1917), 20-41.

3 STEELE, I. K. *Politics of Colonial Policy: The Board of Trade in Colonial Administration 1696-1720*. Oxford, 1968.

Other Departments

4 BENNETT, J. H. "English Bishops and Imperial Jurisdiction, 1660-1725." *Hist Mag P E Ch*, XXXII (1963), 175-188.

5 CLARK, Dora Mae. *The Rise of the British Treasury; Colonial Administration in the 18th Century*. New Haven, 1960.

6 CROSS, Arthur L. *The Anglican Episcopate and the American Colonies*. New York, 1902.

7 DOTY, Joseph D. *The British Admiralty Board as a Factor in Colonial Administration, 1689-1763*. Philadelphia, 1930.

8 HOON, Elizabeth E. *The Organization of the English Customs System*. See 4.10.

Colonial Agents

9 APPLETON, Marguerite. "Richard Partridge: Colonial Agent." *N Eng Q*, V (1932), 293-309.

10 BOND, Beverly W. "The Colonial Agency as a Popular Representative." *Pol Sci Q*, XXXV (1920), 372-392.

11 BURNS, James J. *The Colonial Agents of New England*. Washington, D.C., 1935.

12 FREIBERG, Malcolm. "William Bollan: Agent of Massachusetts." *More Books*, XXIII (1949) 43-53, 90 100, 135-146, 168-182, 212-220.

13 HUTSON, James H. "Benjamin Franklin and the Parliamentary Grant for 1758." *Wm Mar Q*, 3rd ser., XXIII (1966), 575-595.

14 KAMMEN, Michael G. *A Rope of Sand: The Colonial Agents, British Politics, and the American Revolution*. Ithaca, 1968.

15 LILY, Edward P. *The Colonial Agents of New York and New Jersey*. Washington, D.C., 1936.

16 LONN, Ella. *The Colonial Agents of the Southern Colonies*. Chapel Hill, 1945.

17 NAMIER, Lewis B. "Charles Garth and his Connections." *Eng Hist Rev*, LIV (1939), 443-470, 632-652.

18 PENSON, Lillian M. *The Colonial Agents of the British West Indies: A Study in Colonial Administration, Mainly in the Eighteenth Century*. London, 1924.

19 TANNER, Edwin P. "Colonial Agencies in England during the Eighteenth Century." *Pol Sci Q*, XVI (1901), 24-49.

20 VARGA, Nicholas. "Robert Charles, New York Agent, 1748-1770." *Wm Mar Q*, 3rd ser., XVIII (1961), 211-235.

21 WILKINSON, Norman B. "The Colonial Voice in London." *Historian*, III (1940), 22-36.

1 WOLFF, Mabel P. *The Colonial Agency of Pennsylvania, 1712-1757.* Philadelphia, 1933.

POLICY AND ADMINISTRATION

General

2 ALVORD, Clarence W. *The Mississippi Valley in British Politics: A Study of the Trade, Land Speculation, and Experiments in Imperialism Culminating in the American Revolution.* Cleveland, 1917.

3 BARROW, Thomas C. "Background to the Grenville Program, 1757-1763." *Wm Mar Q, 3rd ser.,* XXII (1965), 93-104.

4 BARROW, Thomas C. "A Project for Imperial Reform: 'Hints Respecting the Settlement for our American Provinces,' 1763." *Wm Mar Q,* 3rd ser., XXIV (1967), 108-126.

5 BEER, George L. *British Colonial Policy, 1754-1765.* New York, 1907.

6 BUMSTED, John M. "Doctor Douglass' *Summary:* Polemic for Reform." *N Eng Q,* XXXVII (1964), 242-250.

7 *An Essay upon the Government of the English Plantations on the Continent of America (1701): An Anonymous Virginian's Proposals for Liberty under the British Crown, with Two Memoranda by William Byrd.* Ed. Louis B. Wright. San Marino, Calif., 1945.

8 GRANT, William L. "Canada Versus Guadeloupe, an Episode of the Seven Years' War." *Am Hist Rev,* XVII (1912), 735-743.

9 GRANT, William L. *The Colonial Policy of Chatham.* Kingston, Ont., 1911.

10 GUTTRIDGE, G. H. *The Colonial Policy of William III in America and The West Indies.* Cambridge, Eng., 1922

11 HAFFENDEN, Philip S. "Colonial Appointments and Patronage under the Duke of Newcastle, 1724-1739." *Eng Hist Rev,* LXXVIII (1963), 417-435.

12 HALL, Michael G. *Edward Randolph and the American Colonies, 1676-1703.* Chapel Hill, 1960.†

13 "Hints Relative to the Division and Government of the Conquered and Newly Acquired Countries in America." Ed. Verner W. Crane. *Miss Val Hist Rev,* VIII (1922), 367-373.

14 JACOBSEN, Gertrude A. *William Blathwayt, a Late Seventeenth Century English Administrator.* New Haven, 1932.

15 KIMBALL, Everett. *The Public Life of Joseph Dudley, A Study of the Colonial Policy of the Stuarts in New England, 1660-1715.* New York, 1911.

16 KNOLLENBERG, Bernhard. *Origin of the American Revolution, 1759-1766.* Rev. ed. New York, 1965.†

17 LOKKEN, Roy N. "Sir William Keith's Theory of the British Empire." *Historian,* XXV (1963), 403-418.

18 "Martin Bladen's Blueprint for a Colonial Union." Ed. Jack P. Greene. *Wm Mar Q, 3rd ser.,* XVII (1960), 516-530.

19 MULLETT, Charles F. "James Abercromby and French Encroachments in America." *Canada Hist Rev,* XXVI (1945), 48-59.

20 POWNALL, Thomas. *The Administration of the Colonies, wherein their Rights and Constitutions are Discussed and Stated.* London, 1764.

1 SOSIN, Jack M. *Whitehall and the Wilderness: The Middle West in British Colonial Policy, 1760-1775.* Lincoln, Neb., 1961.

2 SOUTHWICK, Albert B. "The Molasses Act – Source of Precedents." *Wm Mar Q, 3rd ser.,* VIII (1951), 389-405.

3 WICKWIRE, Franklin B. *British Subministers and Colonial America, 1763-1783.* Princeton, 1966.

4 WICKWIRE, Franklin B. "John Pownall and British Colonial Policy." *Wm Mar Q,* 3rd ser., XX (1963), 543-555.

Administration and Enforcement

5 BARROW, Thomas C. *Trade and Empire: The British Customs Service in Colonial America 1660-1775.* Cambridge, Mass., 1967.

6 BINING, Arthur C. *British Regulation of the Colonial Iron Industry.* Philadelphia, 1933.

7 DICKERSON, Oliver M. *The Navigation Acts and the American Revolution.* Philadelphia 1951.†

8 GREENE, Evarts B. *The Provincial Governor in the English Colonies of North America.* New York, 1898.

9 HARPER, Lawrence A. "The Effect of the Navigation Acts on the Thirteen Colonies." In *The Era of the American Revolution,* ed. Richard B. Morris. New York, 1939 †

10 HARPER, Lawrence A. *The English Navigation Laws; A Seventeenth-Century Experiment in Social Engineering.* New York, 1939.

11 HARPER, Lawrence A. "Mercantilism and the American Revolution." *Canad Hist Rev,* XXIII (1942), 1-16.

12 JUDAH, Charles B., Jr. *The North American Fisheries and British Policy to 1713.* Urbana, Ill., 1933.

13 LABAREE, Leonard W. *Royal Government in America, A Study of the British Colonial System before 1783.* New Haven 1930.

14 LAWSON, Murray G. *Fur: A Study in English Mercantilism, 1700-1775.* Toronto, 1943.

15 NETTELS, Curtis P. "British Mercantilism and the Economic Development of the Thirteen Colonies." *J Econ Hist,* XII (1952), 105-114.

16 NETTELS, Curtis P. "The Menace of Colonial Manufacturing, 1690-1720." *N Eng Q,* IV (1931), 230-269.

17 NETTELS, Curtis P. "The Place of Markets in the Old Colonial System." *N Eng. Q,* VI (1933), 491-512.

18 RANSOM, Roger L. "British Policy and Colonial Growth: Some Implications of the Burden from the Navigation Acts." *J Econ Hist,* XXVIII (1968), 427-435.

19 ROOT, Winfred T. *The Relations of Pennsylvania with the British Government, 1696-1765.* Philadelphia, 1912.

20 SHERIDAN, Richard B. "The Wealth of Jamaica in the Eighteenth Century: A Rejoinder." *Econ Hist Rev,* 2nd ser., XXI (1968), 46-61.

21 SIOUSSAT, St. George Leakin. "Virginia and the English Commercial System, 1730-1733." *Am Hist Assn Ann Rep,* I (1905), 71-97.

22 STRICKLAND, Reba C. "The Mercantile System as Applied to Georgia." *Ga Hist Q,* XXII (1938), 160-168.

1 THOMAS, Robert Paul. "A Quantitative Approach to the Study of the Effects of British Imperial Policy upon Colonial Welfare: Some Preliminary Findings." *J Econ Hist,* XVIII, (1965), 615-638.

2 THOMAS, Robert Paul. "British Imperial Policy and the Economic Interpretation of the American Revolution." *J Econ Hist,* XXVIII (1968), 436-440.

3 THOMAS, Robert Paul. "The Sugar Colonies of the Old Empire: Profit or Loss for Great Britain?" *Econ Hist Rev,* 2nd ser, XXI (1968), 30-45.

4 UBBELOHDE, Carl. *The Vice-Admiralty Courts and the American Revolution.* Chapel Hill, 1960.

5 WROTH, L. K. "The Massachusetts Vice-Admiralty Court," in *Law and Authority in Colonial America.* Ed. George A. Billias. Barre, Mass., 1965.

Naval Stores and Forest Policy

6 ALBION, R. G. *Forests and Seapower: The Timber Problem of the Royal Navy, 1652-1862.* Cambridge, Mass., 1926.

7 CARLTON, William R. "New England Masts and the King's Navy." *N Eng Q,* XII (1939), 4-18.

8 KNITTLE, Walter A. *The Early Eighteenth Century Palatine Emigration; A British Government Redemptioner Project to Manufacture Naval Stores.* Philadelphia, 1936.

9 LORD, Eleanor L. *Industrial Experiments in the British Colonies of North America.* Baltimore, 1898.

10 MALONE, Joseph J. *Pine Trees and Politics: The Naval Stores and Forest Policy in Colonial New England, 1691-1775.* Seattle, 1964.

11 WILLIAMS, Justin. "English Mercantilism and Carolina Naval Stores, 1705-1776." *J S Hist,* I (1935), 169-185.

Relationships with Proprietary and Charter Colonies

12 BURANELLI, Vincent. *The King and the Quakers: A Study of William Penn and James II.* Philadelphia, 1962.

13 CRITTENDEN, Charles C. "The Surrender of the Charter of Carolina." *N C Hist Rev,* I (1924), 383-402.

14 ILLICK, Joseph E. *William Penn the Politician: His Relations with The English Government.* Ithaca, 1965.

15 KELLOGG, Louise P. *The American Colonial Charter: A Study of English Administration in Relation thereto, Chiefly after 1688.* Washington, D.C., 1904.

16 OLSON, Alison G. "William Penn, Parliament, and Proprietary Government." *Wm Mar Q,* 3rd ser., XVIII (1961), 176-195.

17 STEELE, I. K. "The Board of Trade, the Quakers, and Resumption of Colonial Charters, 1699-1702." *Wm Mar Q,* 3rd ser., XXIII (1966), 596-619.

The Establishment of Georgia

18 CHURCH, Leslie F. *Oglethorpe: A Study of Philanthropy in England and Georgia.* London, 1932.

1 CRANE, Verner W. "Dr. Thomas Bray and the Charitable Colony Project, 1730." *Wm Mar Q,* 3rd ser., XIX (1962), 49-64.

2 CRANE, Verner W. "Projects for Colonization in the South, 1684-1732." *Miss Val Hist Rev,* XII (1925), 23-35.

3 DUNN, Richard S. "The Trustees of Georgia and the House of Commons, 1732-1752." *Wm Mar Q,* 3rd ser., XI (1954), 551-565.

4 ETTINGER, Amos A. *James Edward Oglethorpe, Imperial Idealist.* Oxford, 1936.

5 MERONEY, Geraldine. "The London Entrepot Merchants and the Georgia Colony." *Wm Mar Q,* 3rd ser., XXV (1968), 230-244.

6 REESE, Trevor R. *Colonial Georgia: A Study in British Imperial Policy in the Eighteenth Century.* Athens, Ga., 1963.

7 REESE, Trevor R. "Religious Factors in the Settlement of a Colony: Georgia in the Eighteenth Century." *J Rel Hist,* I (1961), 206-216.

The Movement for Union Prior to the Seven Years' War

8 MATHEWS, Lois K. "Benjamin Franklin's Plans for a Colonial Union, 1750-1775." *Am Pol Sci Rev,* VIII (1914), 393-412.

9 MORRIS, Richard B. "Benjamin Franklin's Grand Design. The Albany Plan of Union Might have made the Revolution Unnecessary." *Am Her,* VII (1956), 4-7, 106-109.

10 NEWBOLD, Robert C. *The Albany Congress and Plan of Union of 1754.* New York, 1955.

11 OLSON, Alison G. "The British Government and Colonial Union, 1754." *Wm Mar Q,* XVII (1960), 22-34.

Competition for Empire

DIPLOMATIC RIVALRY

12 GILBERT, Felix. "The English Background of American Isolationism in the Eighteenth Century." *Wm Mar Q,* 3rd ser., I (1944), 138-160.

13 HILDNER, Ernest G., Jr. "The Role of the South Sea Company in the Diplomacy Leading to the War of Jenkins' Ear, 1729-1739." *His—Am Hist Rev,* XVIII (1938), 322-341.

14 JOHNSON, James G. "The Colonial Southeast, 1732-1763; An International Contest for Territorial and Economic Control." *U Colo Stud,* XIX, No. 3 (1932), 163-226.

15 LANNING, John Tate. *The Diplomatic History of Georgia; A Study of the Epoch of Jenkins' Ear.* Chapel Hill, 1936.

16 LONN, Ella. "The French Council of Commerce in Relation to American Trade." *Miss Val Hist Rev,* VI (1919), 192-219.

17 MC LACHLAN, Jean O. *Trade and Peace with Old Spain, 1667-1750 . . . .* Cambridge, Eng., 1940.

18 PARES, Richard. *Colonial Blockade and Neutral Rights, 1739-1763.* Oxford, 1938.

1 PEASE, Theodore C. "The Mississippi Boundary of 1763: A Reappraisal of Responsibility." *Am Hist Rev,* XL (1935), 278-286.

2 RASHED, Zenab E. *The Peace of Paris, 1763.* Liverpool, 1951.

3 REESE, Trevor R. "Georgia in Anglo-Spanish Diplomacy, 1736-1739." *Wm Mar Q,* 3rd ser., XV (1958), 168-190.

4 SAVELLE, Max. "The American Balance of Power and European Diplomacy, 1713-1778," in *The Era of the American Revolution.* Ed. Richard B. Morris. New York, 1939.†

5 SAVELLE, Max. *The Diplomatic History of the Canadian Boundary, 1749-1763.* New Haven, 1940

6 SAVELLE, Max. "Diplomatic Preliminaries of the Seven Years' War in America." *Canad Hist Rev,* XX (1939), 17-36.

7 SAVELLE, Max. "The International Approach to Early Anglo–American History, 1492-1763." In *The Reinterpretation of Early American History: Essays in Honor of John Edwin Pomfret,* ed Ray Allen Billington. San Marino, Calif., 1966.†

8 SAVELLE, Max. *The Origins of American Diplomacy: The International History of Anglo–America, 1492-1763.* New York, 1967.

9 SOSIN, Jack M. "Louisbourg and the Peace of Aix-la-Chapelle, 1748." *Wm Mar Q,* 3rd ser., XIV (1957), 516-535.

10 WILSON, Arthur McCandless. *French Foreign Policy during the Administration of Cardinal Fleury, 1726-1743; A Study in Diplomacy and Commercial Development.* Cambridge, Mass., 1936.

11 ZOLTVANY, Yves. "The Frontier Policy of Phillippe de Regaud de Vaudreuil." *Canad Hist Rev,* XLVIII (1967), 227-250.

MILITARY AND NAVAL CONFLICT

12 ALBERTS, Robert C. *The Most Extraordinary Adventures of Major Robert Stobo.* Boston, 1965.

13 ALDEN, John Richard. *General Gage in America: Being Principally a History of His Role in the American Revolution.* Baton Rouge, 1948.

14 ALVORD, Clarence W. *Illinois Country, 1673-1818.* Springfield, Ill., 1920.

15 BUFFINTON, Arthur H. "The Canada Expedition of 1746; its Relation to British Politics." *Am Hist Rev,* XLV (1940), 552-580.

16 CALDWELL, Norman W. "The Southern Frontier during King George's War." *J S Hist,* VII (1941), 37-54.

17 CRANE, Verner W. *The Southern Frontier, 1670-1732.* Durham N.C., 1928.†

18 DALTON, J. C. "Louisbourg 1745, 1758, an Historical Retrospect." *J Roy Artil,* LV (1929), 478-494.

19 ECCLES, W. J. *Frontenac the Courtier Governor.* Toronto, 1959.†

20 FRÉGAULT, Guy. *La Guerre de la Conquête.* Montreal, 1955.

1   FRÉGAULT, Guy. "L'Empire Britannique et la conquête du Canada, 1700-1713." *Rev Hist Am Fr,* X (1956), 153-182.

2   GRAHAM, Gerald Sanford. "The Naval Defence of British North America, 1739-1763." *Roy Hist Soc Trans,* 4th ser., XXX (1948), 95-110.

3   GRANT, W. L. "The Capture of Oswego by Montcalm in 1756; A Study in Naval Power: . . ." *Roy Soc Canad Trans,* 3rd ser., VIII (1914), 193-214.

4   HAMILTON, Edward P. *The French and Indian Wars; The Story of Battles and Forts in the Wilderness.* Garden City, N.Y., 1962.

5   HIBBERT, Christopher. *Wolfe at Quebec.* Cleveland, 1959.

6   HIGONNET, Patrice Louis-René. "The Origins of the Seven Years' War." *J Mod Hist,* XL(1968), 57-90.

7   LLOYD, Christopher. *The Capture of Quebec.* London, 1959.

8   LEACH, Douglas Edward. *The Northern Colonial Frontier, 1607-1763.* New York, 1966.

9   LONG, John Cuthbert. *Lord Jeffery Amherst, A Soldier of the King.* New York, 1933.

10 LYDON, James G. "The Great Capture of 1744." *N-Y Hist Soc Q.* LII (1968), 255-269.

11 MC CARDELL, Lee. *Ill—Starred General: Braddock of the Coldstream Guards.* Pittsburgh, 1958.

12 MAHON, John K. "Anglo-American Methods of Indian Warfare, 1676-1794." *Miss Val Hist Rev,* XLV (1958), 254-275.

13 MAYO, Lawrence Shaw. *Jeffery Amherst; A Biography.* New York, 1916.

14 MIDDLETON, C. R. "A Reinforcement for North America, Summer 1757" *Bull Inst Hist Res,* XLI (1968), 58-72.

15 MORGAN, William Thomas. "The British West Indies during King William's War (1689-97)." *J Mod Hist, II (1930), 378-409.*

16 MORGAN, William Thomas. *Queen Anne's Canadian expedition of 1711.* Kingston, Ont., 1928.

17 MORGAN, William Thomas. "Some Attempts at Imperial Co—operation during the Reign of Queen Anne." *Roy Hist Soc Trans,* 4th ser., X (1927), 171-194.

18 MULKEARN, Lois. "The English Eye the French in North America." *Pa Hist,* XXI (1954), 316-337.

19 NICHOLS, Franklin Thayer. "The Organization of Braddock's Army." *Wm Mar Q,* 3rd ser., IV (1947), 125-147.

20 PARES, Richard. "American Versus Continental Warfare, 1739-1763." *Eng. Hist Rev,* LI (1936), 429-465.

21 PARES, Richard. "The Manning of the Navy in the West Indies 1702-63." *Roy Hist Soc Trans,* 4th Ser., XX (1937), 31-60.

22 PARES, Richard. *War and Trade in the West Indies, 1739-1763.* Oxford, 1936.

23 PARGELLIS, Stanley. "Braddock's Defeat." *Am Hist Rev,* XLI (1936), 253-269.

1 PARGELLIS, Stanley. "The Four Independent Companies of New York." In *Essays in Colonial History Presented to Charles McLean Andrews. . . .*New Haven, 1931.

2 PARGELLIS, Stanley. *Lord Loudoun in North America.* New Haven, 1933.

3 PARGELLIS, Stanley. *Military Affairs in North America, 1748-1765: Selected Documents from the Cumberland Papers in Windsor Castle.* New York, 1936.

4 PECKHAM, Howard H. *The Colonial Wars, 1689-1762.* Chicago, 1964.†

5 PHELPS, Dawson A. "The Vaudreuil Expedition, 1752." *Wm Mar Q,* 3rd ser., XV (1958), 483-493.

6 PRIESTLY, Herbert I. *France Overseas through the Old Régime; A Study of European Expansion.* New York, 1939.

7 POIRIER, Pascal. *Des Acadiens Déportés à Boston, en 1755.* Ottawa, 1909.

8 RAMSEY, Russell W. "The Defeat of Admiral Vernon at Cartagena in 1741." *S Q,* I (1963), 332-355.

9 RAWLYK, G. A. *Yankees at Louisbourg.* Orono, Me., 1967.

10 REESE, Trevor R. "Britain's Military Support of Georgia in the War of 1739-1748." *Ga Hist Q,* XLIII (1959), 1-10.

11 RICHMOND, Herbert William. "Colonial Defence during the War, 1739-48." In his *The Navy in the War of 1739-48.* Vol. III, 268-278. Cambridge, Eng., 1920.

12 RICHMOND, Herbert William. "The Influence of Sea–Power on the Struggle with France in North America and India." *Nat Rev,* LXXV (1920), 397-411.

13 RUTLEDGE, Joseph Lister. *Century of Conflict. The Struggle between the French and British in Colonial America.* Garden City, N.Y., 1956.

14 SCHUTZ, John A. "The Disaster of Fort Ticonderoga: The Shortage of Muskets during the Mobilization of 1758." *Hunt. Lib. Q,* XIV (1951), 307-315.

15 SHAFROTH, John F. "The Capture of Louisbourg in 1758; A Joint Military and Naval Operation." *U S N Inst Proc,* LXIV (1938), 78-96.

16 SMELSER, Marshall. *The Campaign for the Sugar Islands, 1759.* Chapel Hill, 1955.

17 STACEY, C. P. *Quebec, 1759: The Siege and the Battle.* New York, 1959.

18 SYRETT, David. "American Provincials and the Havana Campaign," *N Y Hist,* XLIX (1968), 375-390.

19 TE PASKE, John Jay. *The Governor of Spanish Florida, 1700-1763.* Durham, N.C., 1964.

20 THAYER, Theodore G. "The Army Contractors for the Niagara Campaign, 1755-1756." *Wm Mar Q,* XIV (1957), 31-46.

21 VINER, Jacob. "Power Versus Plenty as Objectives of Foreign Policy in the Seventeenth and Eighteenth Centuries." *Wor Pol,* I (1948). 1-29.

22 WALL, Robert E. Jr. "Louisbourg, 1745." *N Eng Q,* XXXVII (1964), 64-83.

23 WALLER, G. M. *Samuel Vetch: Colonial Enterpriser.* Chapel Hill, 1960.

24 WINZERLING, Oscar W. *Acadian Odyssey.* Baton Rouge, 1955.

25 WOOD, William C. H. *The Great Fortress; a Chronicle of Louisbourg, 1720-1760.* Toronto, 1915.

1 WOOD, George A. "Céloron de Blainville and French Expansion in the Ohio Valley." *Miss Val Hist Rev,* IX (1923), 302-319.

2 ZÓLTVANY, Yves F. "New France and the West, 1701-1713." *Canad Hist Rev,* XLVI (1965), 301-322.

INDIAN RELATIONS

3 ALDEN, John R. "The Albany Congress and the Creation of the Indian Superintendencies." *Miss Val Hist Rev.* XXVII (1940), 193-210.

4 ALDEN, John R. *John Stuart and the Southern Colonial Frontier: A Study of Indian Relations, War, Trade, and Land Problems in the Southern Wilderness, 1754-1775.* Ann Arbor, 1944.

5 ATKIN, Edmond. *Indians of the Southern Colonial Frontier: The Edmond Atkin Report and Plan of 1755.* Ed. by Wilbur R. Jacobs. Columbia, S.C., 1954.

6 COLDEN, Cadwallader. *The History of the Five Indian Nations of Canada which are Dependent on the Province of New York, and are a Barrier between the English and the French in that Part of the World. . . .* 2 vols. New York, 1902.†

7 CORKRAN, David H. *Cherokee Frontier: Conflict and Survival, 1740-1762.* Norman, Okla., 1962.

8 CORKRAN, David H. *The Creek Frontier, 1540-1783.* Norman, Okla., 1967.

9 CORRY, John Pitts. *Indian Affairs in Georgia, 1732-1756.* Philadelphia, 1936.

10 FLEXNER, James T. *Mohawk Baronet: Sir William Johnson of New York.* New York, 1959.

11 JACOBS, Wilbur R. *Diplomacy and Indian Gifts: Anglo-French Rivalry Along the Ohio and Northwest Frontiers, 1748-1763.* Stanford, Calif., 1950.

12 JACOBS, Wilbur R. "Wampum, The Protocol of Indian Diplomacy." *Wm Mar Q,* 3rd ser., VI (1949), 596-604.

13 MORGAN, William T. "The Five Nations and Queen Anne." *Miss Val Hist Rev,* XIII (1926), 167-189.

14 PECKHAM, Howard H. *Pontiac and the Indian Uprising.* Princeton, 1947.

15 PHELPS, Dawson A. "The Chickasaw, the English, and the French, 1699-1744." *Tenn Hist Q,* XVI (1957), 117-133.

16 POUND, Arthur. *Johnson of the Mohawks; a Biography of Sir William Johnson. . .* New York, 1930.

17 SMOYER, Stanley C. "Indians as Allies in the Intercolonial Wars." *N Y Hist,* XVII (1936), 411-422.

18 WALDON, Freda F. "Queen Anne and 'The Four Kings of Canada'; a Bibliography of Contemporary Sources." *Canad Hist Rev,* XVI (1935), 266-275.

19 WALLACE, Anthony F. C. *King of the Delawares: Teedyuscung, 1700-1763.* Philadelphia, 1949.

20 WALLACE, Anthony F. C. "Origins of Iroquois Neutrality: The Grand Settlement of 1701." *Pa Hist,* XXIV (1957), 223-235.

The Colonies

General

COMPREHENSIVE STUDIES

1   ADAMS, James Truslow. *Provincial Society, 1690-1763*. New York, 1927.

2   ANDREWS, Charles M. *The Colonial Period*. New York, 1912.

3   ANDREWS, Charles M. *The Colonial Period of American History*. 4 vols. New Haven, 1934-1938.†

4   ANDREWS, Charles M. "On the Writing of Colonial History." *Wm Mar Q*, I (1944), 27-48.

5   BOORSTIN, Daniel J. *The Americans: The Colonial Experience*. New York, 1958.†

6   *The Cambridge History of the British Empire*. Ed. J. Holland Rose, A. P. Newton, and E. A. Benians. vol. I, *The Old Empire from the Beginnings to 1783*. Cambridge, Eng., 1929.

7   CHALMERS, George. *An Introduction to the History of the Revolt of the American Colonies; . . . .* 2 vols. Boston, 1845.

8   CHANNING, Edward. *A History of the United States*. vol. II, *A Century of Colonial History, 1660-1760*. New York, 1908.

9   CRAVEN, Wesley Frank. *The Colonies in Transition 1660-1761*. New York, 1968.

10   GIPSON, Lawrence Henry. *The British Empire Before the American Revolution*. 14 vols. New York, 1936-1969.

11   GREENE, Evarts B. *Provincial America, 1690-1740*. New York, 1905.

12   GREENE, Jack P., ed. *Settlements to Society*. vol. I, *A Documentary History of American Life*. New York, 1966.†

13   JENSEN, Merrill, ed. *English Historical Documents: American Colonial Documents, 1607-1776*. New York, 1955.

14   NETTELS, Curtis P. *The Roots of American Civilization; A History of American Colonial Life*. New York, 1938.

15   OSGOOD, Herbert L. *The American Colonies in the Eighteenth Century*. 4 vols. New York, 1924.

16   SCHLESINGER, Arthur M. *The Birth of a Nation: A Portrait of the American People on the Eve of Independence*. New York, 1968.

17   VER STEEG, Clarence L. *The Formative Years, 1607-1763*. New York, 1964.

18   WINSOR, Justin, ed. *Narrative and Critical History of America*. vol. V, *The English and French in North America 1689-1763*. Boston, 1887.

1   WRIGHT, Louis B. *The Atlantic Frontier: Colonial American Civilization, 1607-1763.* New York, 1947.†

STATE AND REGIONAL HISTORIES

2   ABBOT, W. W. "A Cursory View of Eighteenth-Century Georgia." *S Atl Q,* LXI (1962), 339-344.

3   ADAMS, James Truslow. *Revolutionary New England, 1691-1776.* Boston, 1923.

4   ARNOLD, Samuel Greene. *History of the State of Rhode Island and Providence Plantations.* 2 vols., New York, 1859-1860.

5   BELKNAP, Jeremy. *The History of New-Hampshire.* 3 vols. Boston, 1792.

6   BOLLES, Albert Sydney. *Pennsylvania: Province and State. A History from 1609 to 1790.* 2 vols. Philadelphia, 1898.

7   BREBNER, John Bartlet. *The Neutral Yankees of Nova Scotia: A Marginal Colony During the Revolutionary Years.* New York, 1937.

8   BREBNER, John Bartlet. *New England's Outpost: Acadia Before the Conquest of Canada.* New York, 1927.

9   BRONNER, Edwin B. *William Penn's 'Holy Experiment': The Founding of Pennsylvania, 1681-1701.* New York, 1962.

10 BUCK, Solon J. and Elizabeth Hawthorn PECK. *The Planting of Civilization in Western Pennsylvania.* Pittsburgh, 1939.

11 BURNS, Sir Alan C. *History of the British West Indies.* New York, 1954.

12 COULTER, Ellis Merton. *A Short History of Georgia.* Chapel Hill, 1933.

13 CRAVEN, Wesley Frank. *New Jersey and the English Colonization of North America.* Princeton, 1964.

14 FLICK, Alexander C., ed. *History of the State of New York.* 4 vols. New York, 1933.

15 HART, Albert Bushnell, ed. *Commonwealth History of Massachusetts.* vol. II, *Province of Massachusetts (1689-1775).* New York, 1928.

16 HUTCHINSON, Thomas. *The History of the Colony and Province of Massachusetts Bay.* 3 vols. Cambridge, Mass., 1936.

17 LEE, Lawrence. *The Lower Cape Fear in Colonial Days.* Chapel Hill, 1965.

18 LEFLER, Hugh T. and Albert Ray NEWSOME. *North Carolina: The History of a Southern State.* Chapel Hill, 1954.

19 MC CORMICK, Richard P. *New Jersey from Colony to State, 1609-1789.* Princeton, 1964.

20 MORTON, Richard L. *Colonial Virginia:* vol. I, *The Tidewater Period, 1607-1710;* vol. II, *Westward Expansion and Prelude to Revolution, 1710-1763.* Chapel Hill, 1960.

21 POMFRET, John E. *The Province of East New Jersey, 1609-1702: The Rebellious Proprietary.* Princeton, 1962.

1   POMFRET, John E. *The Province of West New Jersey, 1609-1702: A History of the Origins of an American Colony.* Princeton, 1956.

2   SCHARF, John Thomas. *History of Delaware, 1609-1888.* 2 vols. Philadelphia, 1888.

3   SMITH, Samuel. *History of the Colony of Nova-Caesaria or New Jersey to the Year 1721.* Burlington, N.J., 1765.

4   SMITH, William. *History of the Late Province of New York, from its Discovery to 1762.* N-Y Hist Soc Coll, 4-5 (1829-1830).

5   WALLACE, David D. *The History of South Carolina.* 4 vols. New York, 1934-1935.

BIOGRAPHY

Collective

6   DEXTER, Franklin B. *Biographical Sketches of the Graduates of Yale College.* . . .New York, 1885-   .

7   *Dictionary of American Biography, under the Auspices of the American Council of Learned Societies.* . . . New York, 1928-   .

8   *Dictionary of National Biography.* Ed. Leslie Stephen and others. 63 vols. London, 1885-1901.

9   *Sibley's Harvard Graduates; Biographical Sketches of Those who Attended Harvard College . . . with Biographical and other Notes.* Vol. I-   . Boston, 1873-   . (Title Varies.)

Individual

10 ALDRIDGE, Alfred Owen. *Benjamin Franklin, Philosopher and Man.* Philadelphia, 1965.

11 ALDRIDGE, Alfred Owen. *Jonathan Edwards.* New York, 1966.†

12 BEATTY, Richmond Croom. *William Byrd of Westover.* Boston, 1932.

13 BOAS, Ralph and Louise. *Cotton Mather, Keeper of the Puritan Conscience.* New York, 1928.

14 BROWN, William Howard. *Colonel John Goffe, Eighteenth Century New Hampshire.* Manchester, N.H., 1950.

15 CLARKE, Hermann F. and Henry W. FOOTE. *Jeremiah Dummer, Colonial Craftsman and Merchant, 1645-1718.* Boston, 1935.

16 CRANE, Verner W. *Benjamin Franklin and a Rising People.* Boston, 1954.†

17 CRANE, Verner W. *Benjamin Franklin, Englishman and American.* Baltimore, 1936.

18 CUMMINGS, Hubertis. *Richard Peters, Provincial Secretary and Cleric, 1704-1776.* Philadelphia, 1944.

19 DOBREE, Bonamy. *William Penn, Quaker and Pioneer.* London, 1934.

20 FOX, Dixon Ryan. *Caleb Heathcote, Gentleman Colonist; The Story of a Career in the Province of New York, 1692-1721.* New York, 1926.

21 FREEMAN, Douglas Southall. *George Washington: A Biography.* Vols. I & II, *Young Washington.* New York, 1948.

22 GEGENHEIMER, Albert Frank. *William Smith: Educator and Churchman, 1727-1803.* Philadelphia, 1943.

23 GIPSON, Lawrence Henry. *Jared Ingersoll: A Study of American Loyalism.* New Haven, 1920.

1 KNOLLENBERG, Bernhard. *George Washington: The Virginia Period, 1732-1775.* Durham, N.C., 1964.

2 MC GRAIL, Thomas Henry. *The Life of William Alexander, First Earl of Stirling.* Ithaca, 1936.

3 MAYS, David John. *Edmund Pendleton, 1721-1803: A Biography.* Cambridge, Mass., 1952.

4 MILLER, Perry. *Jonathan Edwards.* New York, 1949.†

5 MURDOCK, Kenneth Ballard. *Increase Mather, the Foremost American Puritan.* Cambridge, Mass., 1925.

6 PARKES, Henry Bamford. *Jonathan Edwards, the Fiery Puritan.* New York, 1930.

7 PEARE, Catherine Owens. *William Penn: A Biography.* Philadelphia, 1957.†

8 SAVELLE, Max. *George Morgan, Colony Builder.* New York, 1932.

9 VAN DOREN, Carl. *Benjamin Franklin.* New York, 1938.†

10 WILSON, Daniel Munro. *John Quincy, Master of Mount Wollaston. . . .* Boston, 1909.

11 WINSLOW, Ola E. *Jonathan Edwards, 1703-1758; A Biography.* New York, 1940.†

12 WINSLOW, Ola E. *Samuel Sewall of Boston.* New York, 1964.

The Environment and the Indians

THE ENVIRONMENT

13 BARROWS, Harlan H. *Lectures on the Historical Geography of the United States. . . .* Ed. William A. Koelsch. Chicago, 1962.

14 BROWN, Ralph H. *Historical Geography of the United States.* New York, 1948.

15 CUMMING, William P. *The Southeast in Early Maps, with an Annotated Check List of Printed and Manuscript Regional and Local Maps of South Eastern North America during the Colonial Period.* Princeton, 1958.

16 MATTHIESEN, Peter. *Wildlife in America.* New York, 1959.†

17 MEINIG, Donald W. "The American Colonial Era: A Geographical Commentary." *Proc Roy Geog Soc* (Austral), LIX (1958), 1-22.

18 MEINIG, Donald W. "The Colonial Period, 1609-1775." *Geography of New York State.* Ed. John H. Thompson. Syracuse, 1966.

19 MERRENS, Harry R. *Colonial North Carolina in the Eighteenth Century: A Study in Historical Geography.* Chapel Hill, 1964.

20 MERRENS, Harry R. "Historical Geography and Early American History." *Wm Mar Q,* 3rd ser., XXII (1965), 529-548.

21 PAULLIN, Charles O. *Atlas of the Historical Geography of the United States.* Washington, D.C., 1932.

THE INDIANS

1   BROWN, John P. *Old Frontiers: The Story of the Cherokee Indians from Earlist Times to the Date of Their Removal to the West, 1838.* Kingsport, Tenn., 1938.

2   COLLIER, John. *The Indians of North America.* New York, 1967.

3   COTTERILL, R. S. *The Southern Indians: The Story of the Civilized Tribes before Removal.* Norman, Okla., 1954.

4   DRIVER, Harold E. *Indians of North America.* Chicago, 1961.†

5   FENTON, William N. *American Indian and White Relations to 1830: Needs and Opportunities for Study.* Chapel Hill, 1957.

6   FENTON, William N. "Collecting Materials for a Political History of the Six Nations." *Proc Am Philos Soc,* XCIII (1949), 233-238.

7   HALLOWELL, Alfred I. "Impact of the American Indian on American Culture." *Am Anthro,* LIX (1957), 201-217.

8   HODGE, Frederick, ed. *Handbook of American Indians North of Mexico.* Smithsonian Institution, Bureau of American Ethnology, Bulletin 30. 2 vols. New York, 1960.

9   HUNT, George T. *The Wars of the Iroquois: A Study in Intertribal Trade Relations.* Madison, Wis., 1940.†

10   LOFTON, John M., Jr. "White, Indian, and Negro Contacts in Colonial South Carolina." *S Ind Stud,* I (1949), 3-12.

11   LURIE, Nancie O. "Indian Cultural Adjustment to European Civilization." In *Seventeenth-Century America: Essays on Colonial History,* ed. James M. Smith. Chapel Hill, 1959.†

12   LYDEKKER, John W. *The Faithful Mohawks.* Cambridge, Eng., 1938.

13   MILLING, Chapman J. *Red Carolinians.* Chapel Hill, 1940.

14   PEARCE, Roy H. "Metaphysics of Indian-Hating." *Ethnohist,* IV (1957), 27-40.

15   PEARCE, Roy H. "The 'Ruines of Mankind': The Indian and the Puritan Mind." *J Hist Ideas,* XIII (1952), 200-217.

16   PEARCE, Roy H. *The Savages of America: A Study of the Indian and the Idea of Civilization.* Baltimore, 1953.

17   ROBINSON, W. Stitt, Jr. "The Legal Status of the Indian in Colonial Virginia." *Va Mag Hist,* LXI (1953), 249-259.

18   SMITH, Hale G. *The European and the Indian. European-Indian Contacts in Georgia and Florida.* Gainesville, Fla., 1956.

19   TOLLES, Frederick B. "Nonviolent Contact: The Quakers and the Indians." *Proc Am Philos Soc,* CVII (1963), 93-101.

20   UNDERHILL, Ruth M. *Red Man's America: A History of the Indians in the United States.* Chicago, 1953.

21   WALLACE, Paul A. W. "The Iroquois: A Brief Outline of their History." *Pa Hist,* XXIII (1956), 15-28.

22   WASHBURN, Wilcomb E. "The Moral and Legal Justification for Dispossessing the Indians." In *Seventeenth-Century America: Essays on Colonial History.* Ed. James M. Smith. Chapel Hill, 1959.†

1   WISSLER, Clark. *The American Indian, an Introduction to the Anthropology of the New World.* 3rd ed. New York, 1938.

2   WISSLER, Clark. *Indians of the United States; Four Centuries of their History and Culture.* New York, 1940.†

The Public World

THE INSTITUTIONAL, CONSTITUTIONAL, AND LEGAL SETTING

General

3   BURNS, John F. *Controversies Between Royal Governors and Their Assemblies in the Northern American Colonies.* Boston, 1923.

4   LABAREE, Leonard W. *Royal Government in America.* See **15**.13.

5   MC LAUGHLIN, Andrew C. *The Foundations of American Constitutionalism.* New York, 1932.†

Studies of Individual Colonies

7   FISHER, Edgar J. *New Jersey as a Royal Province, 1738 to 1776.* New York, 1911.

8   FLIPPIN, Percy Scott. "The Royal Government in Georgia, 1752-1776." *Ga Hist Q,* VIII (1924), 1-37, 81-120, 243-291; IX (1925), 187-245; X (1926), 1-25, 251-276; XII (1928), 326-352; XIII (1929), 128-153.

9   FLIPPIN, Percy Scott. *The Royal Government in Virginia, 1624-1775.* New York, 1919.

10 FRY, William Henry. *New Hampshire as a Royal Province.* New York, 1908.

11 GREENE, Jack P. "South Carolina's Colonial Constitution: Two Proposals for Reform." *S C Hist Mag,* LII (1961), 72-81.

12 KELSICK, Cecil A. "The Constitutional History of the Leewards," *Carib Q,* VI (1960), 177-209.

13 MC CAIN, James Ross. *Georgia as a Proprietary Province: The Execution of a Trust.* Boston, 1917.

14 MEAD, Nelson P. *Connecticut as a Corporate Colony.* Lancaster, Pa., 1906.

15 MERENESS, Newton D. *Maryland as a Proprietary Province.* New York, 1901.

16 RAPER, Charles L. *North Carolina, a Study in English Colonial Government.* New York, 1904.

17 SAYE, Albert B. *A Constitutional History of Georgia, 1732-1945.* Athens, Ga., 1948.

18 SAYE, Albert B. *New Viewpoints in Georgia History.* Athens, Ga., 1943.

19 SHEPHERD, William R. *History of Proprietary Government in Pennsylvania.* New York, 1896.

1 SMITH, William Roy. *South Carolina as a Royal Province, 1719-1776.* New York, 1903.

2 SPENCER, Charles W. "Colonial Wars and Constitutional Development in New York." *Addresses and Sermon Delivered before the Society of Colonial Wars in the State of New York, and Year Book for 1914-1915.* New York, 1915.

3 SPENCER, Charles W. *Phases of Royal Government in New York, 1691-1719.* Columbus, Ohio, 1905.

4 SPENCER, Henry R. *Constitutional Conflict in Provincial Massachusetts. . . .* Columbus, Ohio, 1905.

5 SPURDLE, F. G. *Early West Indian Government: Showing the Progress of Government in Barbados, Jamaica and the Leeward Islands, 1660-1783.* Palmerston North, N.Z., 1963.

6 TANNER, Edwin Platt. *The Province of New Jersey, 1664-1738.* New York, 1908.

7 WALLACE, D. Duncan. *Constitutional History of South Carolina from 1725 to 1775.* Abbeville, S.C., 1906.

8 WHITSON, Agnes M. *The Constitutional Development of Jamaica, 1660-1729.* Manchester, Eng., 1929.

The Executive

9 WILKINSON, Henry. "The Governor, the Council & Assembly in Bermuda during the First Half of the XVIIIth Century." *Berm Hist Q,* II (1945), 69-84.

10 BELLOT, Hugh Hale. "Council and Cabinet in the Mainland Colonies." *Roy Hist Soc Trans,* 5th ser., V (1955), 161-176.

11 GREENE, Evarts B. *The Provincial Governor.* See **15**.8.

12 HIGH, James. "A Facet of Sovereignty: the Proprietary Governor and the Maryland Charter." *Md Hist Mag,* LV (1960), 67-81.

13 MC ANEAR, Beverly, ed. "The Income of the Royal Governors of Virginia." *J S Hist,* XVI (1950), 196-211.

14 NAYLOR, Rex M. "The Royal Prerogative in New York, 1691-1775." *N Y St Hist Assn J,* V (1924), 221-255.

15 PARRY, J. H. "The Patent Offices in the British West Indies." *Eng Hist Rev,* LXIX (1954), 200-225.

Legislative Developments

16 CLARKE, Mary Patterson. *Parliamentary Privilege in the American Colonies.* New Haven, 1943.

17 COOK, Florence. "Procedure in the North Carolina Colonial Assembly, 1731-1770." *N C Hist Rev,* VIII (1931), 258-283.

18 CORRY, John Pitts. "Procedure in the Commons House of Assembly in Georgia." *Ga Hist Q,* XIII (1929), 110-127.

19 GREENE, Jack P. *The Quest for Power: The Lower Houses of Assembly in the Southern Royal Colonies, 1689-1763.* Chapel Hill, 1963.

20 HIGHAM, C. S. S. "The General Assembly of the Leeward Islands." *Eng Hist Rev,* XLI (1926), 190-209, 366-388.

1　LEONARD, Sister Joan de Lourdes. "The Organization and Procedure of the Pennsylvania Assembly, 1682-1776." *Pa Mag Hist*, LXXII (1948), 215-239, 376-412.

2　MILLER, Elmer Isaiah. *The Legislature of the Province of Virginia, Its Internal Development*. New York, 1907.

3　MORAN, Thomas F. *The Rise and Development of the Bicameral System in America*. Baltimore, 1895.

4　PARGELLIS, Stanley M. "The Procedure of the Virginia House of Burgesses." *Wm Mar Q*, 2nd ser., VII (1927), 73-86, 143-157.

5　RILEY, Elihu S. *A History of the General Assembly of Maryland, 1635-1904*. Baltimore, 1905.

6　SHILSTONE, E. M. "The Evolution of the General Assembly of Barbados." *Barb Mus Hist Soc J*, I (1934), 187-191.

7　YOUNG, Chester Raymond. "The Evolution of the Pennsylvania Assembly, 1682-1748." *Pa Hist*, XXXV (1968), 147-168.

The Judiciary

8　CHITWOOD, Oliver P. *Justice in Colonial Virginia*. Baltimore, 1905.

9　CHUMBLEY, George Lewis. *Colonial Justice in Virginia; the Development of Judicial System, Typical Laws and Cases of the Period*. Richmond, 1938.

10　LLOYD, William H., Jr. "The Courts of Pennsylvania in the Eighteenth Century Prior to the Revolution." *U Pa Law Rev*, LVI (1908), 28-51.

11　MORRIS, Richard B. "Judicial Supremacy and the Inferior Courts in the American Colonies." *Pol Sci Q*, LV (1940), 429-434.

12　PARKER, Herbert. *Courts and Lawyers of New England*. 4 vols. New York, 1931.

13　PYNCHON, William. *Colonial Justice in Western Massachusetts (1639-1702): The Pynchon Court Record, An Original Judges' Diary of the Administration of Justice in the Springfield Courts in the Massachusetts Bay Colony*. Ed. Joseph H. Smith. Cambridge, Mass., 1961.

14　RANKIN, Hugh F. *Criminal Trial Proceedings in the General Court of Colonial Virginia*. Williamsburg, 1965.

15　RANKIN, Hugh F. "The General Court of Colonial Virginia: Its Jurisdiction and Personnel." *Va Mag Hist*, LXX (1962), 142-153.

16　SETARO, Franklyn C. "The Surrogate's Court of New York: Its Historical Antecedents." *N Y Law Forum*, II (1956), 283-304.

17　STAUFFER, Oliver L. *The Origin of Pennsylvania's Present-Day Courts in Early Colonial Times and a Famous Lawyer and the Zenger Trial*. Philadelphia, 1939.

18　SURRENCY, Erwin C. "The Courts in the American Colonies." *Am J Leg Hist*, XI (1967), 253-276, 347-376.

19　WOODRUFF, Edwin H. "Chancery in Massachusetts." *Bos U Law Rev*, IX (1929), 168-192.

Local Government

20　BOYD, Julian P. "The Sheriff in Colonial North Carolina." *N C Hist Rev*, V (1928), 151-180.

1 DIAMONDSTONE, Judith M. "Philadelphia; Municipal Corporation, 1701-1776." *Pa Mag Hist,* XC (1966), 183-201.

2 EDWARDS, George W. *New York as an Eighteenth Century Municipality, 1731-1776.* New York, 1917.

3 FERGUSON, Isabel. "Country Courts in Virginia, 1700-1830." *N C Hist Rev,* VIII (1931), 14-40.

4 GRIFFITH, Ernest S. *History of American City Governemnt: The Colonial Period.* New York, 1938.

5 GUESS, William C. "County Government in Colonial North Carolina." *James Sprunt Hist Stud,* XI (1911), 5-39.

6 LABAREE, Benjamin W. "New England Town Meeting." *Am Archiv,* XXV (1962), 165-172.

7 MC CAIN, Paul M. *The County Court in North Carolina Before 1750.* Durham, N.C., 1954.

8 PETERSON, Arthur Everett. *New York as an Eighteenth Century Municipality Prior to 1731.* New York, 1917.

9 PORTER, Albert O. *County Government in Virginia.* New York, 1947.

10 SEILER, William H. "The Anglican Parish in Virginia." *Seventeenth-Century America: Essays in Colonial History.* Ed. James M. Smith. Chapel Hill, 1959.†

11 SEYBOLT, R. F. *The Colonial Citizen of New York City; a Comparative Study of Certain Aspects of Citizenship Practice in Fourteenth Century England and Colonial New York City.* Madison, Wis., 1918.

12 SLY, John F. *Town Government in Massachusetts (1620-1930).* Cambridge, Mass., 1930.

13 WALKER, Leola O. "Officials in the City Government of Colonial Williamsburg." *Va Mag Hist,* LXXV (1967), 35-51.

14 WATSON, Alan D. "Regulation and Administration of Roads and Bridges in Colonial Eastern North Carolina." *N C Hist Rev,* XLV (1968), 399-417.

Military Organization

15 BOORSTIN, Daniel J. *The Americans: The Colonial Experience.* See **22.5.**

16 COLE, David. "A Brief Outline of the South Carolina Colonial Militia System." *S C Hist Assn Proc,* 1954 (1955), 14-23.

17 DE VALINGER, Leon. *Colonial Military Organization in Delaware, 1638-1776.* Wilmington, 1938.

18 EKIRCH, Arthur A., Jr. *The Civilian and the Military.* New York, 1956.

19 QUARLES, Benjamin. "The Colonial Militia and Negro Manpower." *Miss Val Hist Rev,* XLV (1959), 643-652.

20 RADABAUGH, Jack S. "The Militia of Colonial Massachusetts." *Mil Affairs,* XXVIII (1954), 1-18.

21 SCISCO, Louis D. "Evolution of Colonial Militia in Maryland." *Md Hist Mag,* XXXV (1940), 166-177.

22 SHARP, Morison. "Leadership and Democracy in the Early New England System of Defense." *Am Hist Rev,* L (1945), 244-260.

1   SHY, John W. "A New Look at Colonial Militia." *Wm Mar Q,* 3rd ser., XX (1963), 175-185.

Financial Administration and Taxation

2   BOND, Beverly N. *The Quit-Rent System in the American Colonies.* New Haven, 1919.

3   DAUGHERTY, Martin M. *Early Colonial Taxation in Delaware.* Wilmington, 1938.

4   FLIPPIN, Percy Scott. *The Financial Administration of the Colony of Virginia.* Baltimore, 1915.

5   GIPSON, Lawrence H. *Studies in Colonial Connecticut Taxation: 1. The Taxation of the Connecticut Towns, 1750-1775. 2. Connecticut Taxation and Parliamentary Aid Preceding the Revolutionary War.* Lehigh University. The Institute of Research. (Circular no.65.) Bethlehem, Pa., 1931, 284-298, 721-739.

6   KAY, Marvin L. "Provincial Taxes in North Carolina during the Administration of Dobbs and Tryon." *N C Hist Rev,* XLII (1965), 440-453.

7   MC ANEAR, Beverly. "Mr. Robert R. Livingston's Reasons Against a Land Tax." *J Pol Econ,* XLVIII (1940), 63-90.

8   PARKER, Coralie. *The History of Taxation in North Carolina during the Colonial Period, 1663-1776.* New York, 1928.

9   RIPLEY, William. *The Financial History of Virginia, 1609-1776. . . .* New York, 1938.

10 ROBINSON, Maurice H. *A History of Taxation in New Hampshire.* New York, 1903.

The Law

General

11 BILLIAS, George A., ed. *Law and Authority in Colonial America: Selected Essays.* Barre, Mass., 1965.

12 MORRIS, Richard B. "The Sources of Early American Law: Colonial Period." *W Va Law Q,* XL (1934), 212-223.

13 MORRIS, Richard B. *Studies in the History of American Law, with Special Reference to the Seventeenth and Eighteenth Centuries.* New York, 1930.

14 SMITH, Joseph H. "The Foundations of Law in Maryland: 1634-1715," *Law and Authority in Colonial America: Selected Essays.* Ed. George A. Billias. Barre, Mass., 1965.

Content and Process of the Law

15 CARPENTER, A. H. "Habeas Corpus in the Colonies." *Am Hist Rev,* VIII (1902), 18-27.

16 CHAFEE, Zechariah, Jr. "Colonial Courts and the Common Law." *Proc Mass Hist Soc,* LXVIII (1952), 132-159.

17 CHAPIN, Bradley. "Colonial and Revolutionary Origins of the American Law of Treason." *Wm Mar Q,* 3rd ser., XVII (1960), 3-21.

18 DALZELL, George W. *Benefit of Clergy in America and Related Matters.* Winston-Salem, N.C., 1955.

1 FELLMAN, David. "The European Background of Early American Ideas Concerning Property." *Temple Law Q,* XIV (1940), 497-516.

2 GOEBEL, Julius, Jr. and T. Raymond NAUGHTON. *Law Enforcement in Colonial New York; a Study in Criminal Procedure (1664-1776).* New York, 1944.

3 GOODMAN, Leonard. "Mandamus in the Colonies: The Rise of the Superintending Power of American Courts." *Am J Leg Hist,* I (1957), 308-336; II (1958), 1-34, 129-147.

4 HASKINS, G. L. "The Beginnings of Partible Inheritance in the American Colonies." *Yale Law J,* LI (1942), 1280-1315.

5 JOHNSON, Herbert Alan. *The Law Merchant and Negotiable Instruments in Colonial New York, 1664 to 1730.* Chicago, 1963.

6 KEIM, C. Ray. "Primogeniture and Entail in Colonial Virginia." *Wm Mar Q,* 3rd ser., XXV (1968), 545-586.

7 NELSON, Harold. "Seditious Libel in Colonial America." *Am J Leg Hist,* III (1959), 160-172.

8 PITTMAN, R. Carter. "Judicial Supremacy in America: Its Colonial and Constitutional History." *Ga Bar J,* XVI (1953), 148-165.

9 REINSCH, Paul S. *English Common Law in the Early American Colonies.* Madison, Wis., 1899.

10 RIDDELL, William R. "Early Provincial Legislative Interference with Private Property." *Canad Bar Rev,* XI (1933), 176-180.

11 RIDDELL, William R. "Impeachment in England and English Colonies." *N Y U Law Q Rev,* VII (1930), 702-708.

12 RIDDELL, William R. "Judicial Execution by Burning at the Stake in New York." *Am Bar Assn J,* XV (1929), 373-376.

13 RIDDELL, William R. "Notes on the Pre-Revolutionary Judiciary in English Colonies." *Canad Bar Rev,* XI (1933), 317-324, 376-384.

14 RIDDELL, William R. "Powers of a Colonial Legislature in Impeachment and Contempt." *Proc Royal Soc Canad,* 3rd ser., XXI (1927), 83-90.

15 RYAN, Edward. "Imprisonment for Debt—Its Origin and Repeal." *Va Mag Hist,* XLII (1934), 53-58.

16 SCOTT, Arthur P. *Criminal Law in Colonial Virginia.* Chicago, 1930.

Civil Liberties

17 ALEXANDER, James. *A Brief Narrative of the Case and Trial of John Peter Zenger.* Ed. Stanley N. Katz. Cambridge, Mass., 1963.

18 LEDER, Lawrence H. "The Role of Newspapers in Early America: 'In Defense of Their Own Liberty.'" *Hunt Lib Q,* XXX (1966), 1-16.

19 LEVY, Leonard W. *Legacy of Suppression: Freedom of Speech and Press in Early American History.* Cambridge, Mass., 1960.†

20 LEVY, Leonard W. and Lawrence H. LEDER. "'Exotic Fruit': The Right Against Compulsory Self-Incrimination in Colonial New York." *Wm Mar Q,* 3rd ser., XX (1963), 3-32.

1   MILLER, Helen Hill. *The Case for Liberty.* Chapel Hill, 1965.†

2   MORRIS, Richard B. "Civil Liberties and Jewish Tradition in Early America." *Am Jew Hist Soc Pub,* XLVI (1956), 20-39.

3   PITTMAN, R. Carter. "The Colonial and Constitutional History of the Privilege Against Self-Incrimination in America." *Va Law Rev,* XXI (1935), 763-789.

4   RACKOW, Felix. "The Right to Counsel: English and American Precedents." *Wm Mar Q,* 3rd ser., XI (1954), 3-27.

THE NATURE AND STRUCTURE OF POLITICS

General

5   BAILYN, Bernard. *The Origins of American Politics.* New York, 1968.

6   GREEN, Jack P. "Changing Interpretations of Early American Politics," in *The Reinterpretation of Early American History,* ed. Ray Billington. San Marino, Calif., 1967.†

7   GREENE, Jack P. "The Roles of the Lower Houses of Assembly in Eighteenth-Century Politics." *J S Hist,* XXXVII (1961), 451-474.

8   MURRIN, John M. "The Myths of Colonial Democracy and Royal Decline in Eighteenth-Century America: A Review Essay." *Cithara,* V (1965), 53-69.

The Intellectual Framework

9   BAILYN, Bernard. *The Ideological Origins of the American Revolution.* Cambridge, Mass., 1967.

10   BUCHANAN, John G. "Drumfire from the Pulpit: Natural Law in Colonial Election Sermons of Massachusetts." *Am J·Leg Hist,* XII (1968), 232-244.

11   BUEL, Richard, Jr. "Democracy and the American Revolution: A Frame of Reference." *Wm Mar Q,* 3rd ser., XXI (1964), 165-190.

12   CONNOR, Paul W. *Poor Richard's Politicks: Benjamin Franklin and His New American Order.* New York, 1965.

13   COOK, George A. *John Wise: Early American Democrat.* New York, 1952.

14   DUNN, Mary Maples. *William Penn: Politics and Conscience.* Princeton, 1967.

15   HANLEY, Thomas O'Brien. "Young Mr. Carroll and Montesquieu." *Md Hist Mag,* LXII (1967), 394-418.

16   LEDER, Lawrence H. *Liberty and Authority: Early American Political Ideology 1689-1763.* Chicago, 1968.

17   LOKKEN, Roy N. "The Concept of Democracy in Colonial Political Thought." *Wm Mar Q,* 3rd ser., XVI (1959), 568-580.

18   LYND, Staughton. *Intellectual Origins of American Radicalism.* New York, 1968.

19   POLE, J. R. "Historians and the Problems of Early American Democracy." *Am Hist Rev,* LXVII (1962), 626-646.

20   ROSSITER, Clinton L. *Seedtime of the Republic: The Origin of the American Tradition of Political Liberty.* New York, 1953.†

21   STEARNS, Raymond P. "John Wise of Ipswich was no Democrat in Politics." *Essex Inst Hist Coll,* XCVII (1961), 2-18.

22   STOURZH, Gerald. *Benjamin Franklin and American Foreign Policy.* Chicago, 1954.

1 TOLLES, Frederick B. *Meeting House & Counting House: The Quaker Merchants of Colonial Philadelphia.* Chapel Hill, 1948.†

The Political Process

General Studies of Individual Colonies

2 ABBOT, W. W. *The Royal Governors of Georgia, 1754-1775.* Chapel Hill, 1959.

3 BARKER, Charles A. *The Background of the Revolution in Maryland.* New Haven, 1940.

4 BRIDENBAUGH, Carl. *Seat of Empire: The Political Role of Eighteenth-Century Williamsburg.* Williamsburg, 1950.

5 BUSHMAN, Richard L. *From Puritan to Yankee: Character and the Social Order in Connecticut, 1690-1765.* Cambridge, Mass., 1967.

6 DAVIDSON, Robert L. D. *War Comes to Quaker Pennsylvania, 1682-1756.* New York, 1957.

7 HERSHBERGER, Guy F. "The Pennsylvania Quaker Experiment in Politics, 1682-1756." *Menn Q Rev,* X (1936), 187-221.

8 KATZ, Stanley N. *Newcastle's New York: Anglo-American Politics, 1732-1753.* Cambridge, Mass., 1968.

9 KEMMERER, Donald L. *Path to Freedom: The Struggle for Self-Government in Colonial New Jersey, 1703-1776.* Princeton, 1940.

10 KLEIN, Milton M. "Politics and Personalities in Colonial New York." *N Y Hist,* XLVII (1966), 3-16.

11 LOVEJOY, David S. *Rhode Island Politics and the American Revolution, 1760 1776.* Providence, 1958.

12 METCALF, George. *Royal Government and Political Conflict in Jamaica, 1729-1783.* London, 1965.

13 NASH, Gary B. *Quakers and Politics: Pennsylvania, 1681-1726.* Princeton, 1968.

14 RODNEY, Richard S. "Delaware Under Governor Keith 1717-1726." *Del Hist,* III (1948), 1-25.

15 ROTHERMUND, Dietmar. *The Layman's Progress: Religious and Political Experience in Colonial Pennsylvania, 1740-1770.* Philadelphia, 1962.

16 SHARPLESS, Isaac. *History of Quaker Government in Pennsylvania.* 2 vols. Philadelphia, 1898.

17 SHIPTON, Clifford K. "The Shaping of Revolutionary New England, 1680-1740." *Pol Sci Q,* L (1935), 584-597.

18 SIRMANS, M. Eugene. *Colonial South Carolina: A Political History, 1663-1763.* Chapel Hill, 1966.

19 SYDNOR, Charles S. *Gentlemen Freeholders: Political Practices in Washington's Virginia.* Chapel Hill, 1952.†

20 THAYER, Theodore G. *Pennsylvania Politics and the Growth of Democracy, 1740-1776.* Harrisburg, Pa., 1953.

21 WERTENBAKER, Thomas J. *Give Me Liberty: The Struggle for Self-Government in Virginia.* Philadelphia, 1958.

22 WILKINSON, Henry C. *Bermuda in the Old Empire.* London, 1950.

23 ZEICHNER, Oscar. *Connecticut's Years of Controversy, 1750-1776.* Chapel Hill, 1949.

The Careers of the Governors

1 BURANELLI, Vincent. "Governor Cosby and his Enemies (1732-1736)." *N Y Hist*, XXXVII (1956), 365-387.

2 CLARK, Charles Branch. "The Career of John Seymour, Governor of Maryland, 1704-1709." *Md Hist Mag*, XLVIII (1953), 134-159.

3 CLARKE, Desmond. *Arthur Dobbs, Esquire, 1689-1765: Surveyor-General of Ireland, Prospector, and Governor of North Carolina.* Chapel Hill, 1957.

4 CUNDALL, Frank. *The Governors of Jamaica in the First Half of the 18th Century.* London, 1937.

5 DAVIS, Alice. "The Administration of Benjamin Fletcher in New York." *N Y St Hist Assn J*, II (1921), 213-250.

6 DODSON, Leonidas. *Alexander Spotswood, Governor of Colonial Virginia, 1710-1722.* Philadelphia, 1932.

7 DUNBAR, Louise. "The Royal Governors in the Middle and Southern Colonies on the Eve of the Revolution: A Study in Imperial Personnel," in *The Era of the American Revolution,* ed. Richard B. Morris. New York, 1965.†

8 EDGAR, Matilda Ridout. *A Colonial Governor in Maryland, Horatio Sharpe and His Times, 1753-1773.* London, 1912.

9 FLIPPIN, Percy Scott. "William Gooch: Successful Royal Governor of Virginia." *Wm Mar Q*, 2nd ser., V (1925), 225-258; VI (1926), 1-38; *N C Hist Rev*, IV (1927), 37-49.

10 FREIBERG, Malcolm. "How to Become a Colonial Governor: Thomas Hutchinson of Massachusetts." *Rev Pol*, XXI (1959), 646-656.

11 FREIBERG, Malcolm. "Thomas Hutchinson: The First Fifty Years (1711-1761)." *Wm Mar Q*, 3rd ser., XV (1958), 35-55.

12 GIDDENS, Paul H. "Governor Horatio Sharpe and his Maryland Government." *Md Hist Mag*, XXXII (1937), 156-174.

13 HARLOW, Vincent T. *Christopher Coddrington, 1668-1710.* Oxford, 1928.

14 KEYS, Alice M. *Cadwallader Colden: A Representative Eighteenth Century Official.* New York, 1906.

15 KOONTZ, Louis Knott. *Robert Dinwiddie: His Career in American Colonial Government and Westward Expansion.* Glendale, Calif., 1941.

16 LABAREE, Leonard Woods. "The Early Careers of the Royal Governors," in *Essays in Colonial History Presented to Charles McLean Andrews. . . .* New Haven, 1931.

17 LABAREE, Leonard Woods. "The Royal Governors of New England." *Pub Col Soc Mass*, XXXII (1937), 120-131.

18 PARKER, Charles W. "Lewis Morris, First Colonial Governor of New Jersey." *Proc N J Hist Soc*, XIII (1928), 273-282.

19 SAWTELLE, William Otis. "Thomas Pownall, Colonial Governor, and some of his Activities in the American Colonies." *Proc Mass Hist Soc*, LXIII (1931), 233-284.

20 SCHUTZ, John A. *Thomas Pownall, British Defender of American Liberty: A Study of Anglo-American Relations in the Eighteenth Century.* Glendale, Calif., 1951.

1 SCHUTZ, John A. *William Shirley: King's Governor of Massachusetts.* Chapel Hill, 1961.

2 SHERMAN, Richard P. *Robert Johnson, Proprietary and Royal Governor of South Carolina.* Columbia, S.C., 1966.

3 SPENCER, Charles W. "The Cornbury Legend." *Proc N Y St Hist Assn,* XIII (1914), 309-320.

4 WAINWRIGHT, Nicholas B. "Governor John Blackwell." *Pa Mag Hist,* LXXIV (1950), 457-472.

5 WAINWRIGHT, Nicholas B. "Governor William Denny in Pennsylvania." *Pa Mag Hist,* LXXXI (1957), 170-198.

6 WALETT, Francis G. "Sir William Phips: The First Royal Governor of Massachusetts." *Proc Bos Soc,* (1954), 23-36.

7 WEBB, Stephen S. "The Strange Career of Francis Nicholson." *Wm Mar Q,* 3rd ser., XXIII (1966), 513-548.

8 WOOD, George A. *William Shirley, Governor of Massachusetts, 1741-1756, a History.* New York, 1920.

The Careers of Colonial Politicians

9 DILLON, Dorothy R. *The New York Triumvirate: A Study of the Legal and Political Careers of William Livingston, John Morin Scott, William Smith, Jr.* New York, 1949.

10 DUNN, Richard S. *Puritans and Yankees: The Winthrop Dynasty of New England, 1630-1717.* Princeton, 1962.

11 GERLACH, Don R. *Philip Schuyler and the American Revolution in New York, 1733-1777.* Lincoln, Neb., 1964.

12 HANNA, William S. *Benjamin Franklin and Pennsylvania Politics.* Stanford, Calif., 1964.

13 LAND, Aubrey C. *The Dulanys of Maryland: A Biographical Study of Daniel Dulany the Elder (1685-1753) and Daniel Dulany the Younger (1722-1797).* Baltimore, 1955.

14 LEDER, Lawrence H. *Robert Livingston, 1654-1728, and the Politics of Colonial New York.* Chapel Hill, 1961.

15 LOKKEN, Roy N. *David Lloyd: Colonial Lawmaker.* Seattle, 1959.

16 MAYO, Lawrence S. *The Winthrop Family in America.* Boston, 1948.

17 SHARPLESS, Isaac. *Political Leaders of Provincial Pennsylvania.* New York, 1919.

18 SIOUSSAT, St. George L. *Economics and Politics in Maryland, 1720-1750, and the Public Services of Daniel Dulany the Elder.* Baltimore, 1903.

19 SIRMANS, M. Eugene. "Politicians and Planters: The Bull Family of Colonial South Carolina." *Proc S C Hist Assn,* 1962 (1963), 32-41.

20 THAYER, Theodore. *Israel Pemberton, King of the Quakers.* Philadelphia, 1943.

21 WALLACE, David D. *The Life of Henry Laurens.* New York, 1915.

22 WATERS, John J., Jr. *The Otis Family in Provincial and Revolutionary Massachusetts.* Chapel Hill, 1968.

23 ZIMMERMAN, Albright G. "James Logan, Proprietary Agent." *Pa Mag Hist,* LXXVIII (1954), 143-176.

The Franchise, Elections, and Representation

1 BISHOP, Cortlandt. *History of Elections in the American Colonies.* New York, 1893.

2 BROWN, Robert Eldon. *Middle-Class Democracy and the Revolution in Massachusetts, 1691-1780.* Ithaca, 1955.

3 BROWN, Robert Eldon and B. Katherine. *Virginia, 1705-1786: Democracy or Aristocracy?* East Lansing, Mich., 1964.

4 CARY, John. "Statistical Method and the Brown Thesis on Colonial Democracy." *Wm Mar Q,* 3rd ser., XX (1963), 251-264. (See also Brown's reply, 265-276.)

5 COHEN, Norman S. "The Philadelphia Election Riot of 1742." *Pa Mag Hist,* XCII (1968), 306-319.

6 COLEGROVE, Kenneth. "New England Town Mandates; Instructions to the Deputies in Colonial Legislatures." *Pub Col Soc Mass,* XXI (1920), 411-449.

7 GRANT, Charles S. *Democracy in the Connecticut Frontier Town of Kent.* New York, 1961.

8 KLEIN, Milton M. "Democracy and Politics in Colonial New York." *N Y Hist,* XL (1959), 221-246.

9 LEONARD, Sister Joan de Lourdes. "Elections in Colonial Pennsylvania." *Wm Mar Q,* 3rd ser., XI (1954), 385-401.

10 MC CORMICK, Richard P. *The History of Voting in New Jersey: A Study of the Development of Election Machinery, 1664-1911.* New Brunswick, N.J., 1953.

11 MC KINLEY, Albert E. *The Suffrage Franchise in the Thirteen English Colonies in America.* Philadelphia, 1905.

12 PHILLIPS, Hubert. *The Development of a Residential Qualification for Representatives in Colonial Legislatures.* Cincinnati, 1921.

13 POLE, J. R. *Political Representation in England and the Origins of the American Republic.* New York, 1966.

14 RICH, Robert H. "Election Machinery in New Jersey, 1702-1775." *Proc N J Hist Soc,* LXVII (1949), 198-217.

15 STEINER, Bernard C. *Citizenship and Suffrage in Maryland.* Baltimore, 1895.

16 VARGA, Nicholas. "Election Procedures in Colonial New York." *N Y Hist,* XLI (1960), 249-277.

17 WILLIAMSON, Chilton. *American Suffrage from Property to Democracy, 1760-1860.* Princeton, 1960.

18 ZUCKERMAN, Michael. "The Social Context of Democracy in Massachusetts." *Wm Mar Q,* 3rd ser., XXV (1968), 523-544.

Issues, Divisions, and Conditions of Political Life

19 BAILYN, Bernard. "The Beekmans of New York: Trade, Politics, and Families." *Wm Mar Q,* 3rd ser., XIV (1957), 601-602.

20 BAILYN, Bernard. "Politics and Social Structure in Virginia," in *Seventeenth-Century America: Essays in Colonial History,* ed. James M. Smith. Chapel Hill, 1959.†

21 BILLIAS, George A. *The Massachusetts Land Bankers of 1740.* Orono, Me., 1959.

22 BOYER, Paul S. "Borrowed Rhetoric: The Massachusetts Excise Controversy of 1754." *Wm Mar Q,* 3rd ser., XXI (1964), 328-351.

1 BRENNAN, Ellen E. *Plural Office-Holding in Massachusetts, 1760-1780: Its Relation to the "Separation" of Departments of Government.* Chapel Hill, 1945.

2 BRONNER, Edwin B. "The Disgrace of John Kinsey, Quaker Politician, 1739-1750." *Pa Mag Hist,* LXXV (1951), 400-415.

3 BROWN, Richard M. *The South Carolina Regulators: The Story of the First Vigilante Movement.* Cambridge, Mass., 1963.

4 DANIELL, Jere R. "Politics in New Hampshire Under Governor Benning Wentworth, 1741-1767." *Wm Mar Q,* 3rd ser., XXIII (1966), 76-105.

5 EDWARDS, George W. "New York City Politics before the American Revolution." *Pol Sci Q,* XXXVI (1921), 586-602.

6 ESHLEMAN, H. Frank. "The Struggle and Rise of Popular Power in Pennsylvania's First Two Decades, 1682-1701." *Pa Mag Hist,* XXXIV (1910), 129-161.

7 GLEASON, J. Philip. "A Scurrilous Colonial Election and Franklin's Reputation." *Wm Mar Q,* 3rd ser., XVIII (1961), 68-84.

8 GREENE, Jack P. "The Attempt to Separate the Offices of Speaker and Treasurer in Virginia, 1758-1766." *Va Mag Hist,* LXXI (1963), 11-18.

9 GREENE, Jack P. "Foundations of Political Power in the Virginia House of Burgesses, 1720-1776." *Wm Mar Q,* 3rd ser., X (1959), 485-506.

10 GREENE, Jack P. "The Gadsen Election Controversy and the Revolutionary Movement in South Carolina." *Miss Val Hist Rev,* XLVI (1959), 469-492.

11 GREENE, Jack P. "The North Carolina Lower House and the Power to Appoint Public Treasurers, 1711-1775." *N C Hist Rev,* XL (1963), 37-43.

12 GREENE, Jack P. "The Opposition to Lieutenant Governor Alexander Spotswood, 1718." *Va Mag Hist,* LXX (1962), 35-42.

13 GREENE, Jack P. "The South Carolina Quartering Dispute, 1757-1758." *S C Hist Mag,* L (1959), 193-204.

14 GREENE, Jack P., ed. "The Case of the Pistole Fee: The Report of a Hearing on the Pistole Fee Dispute Before the Privy Council, June 18, 1754." *Va Mag Hist,* LX (1958), 399-422.

15 GRIFFITH, Lucille. *Virginia House of Burgesses, 1750-1774.* North Port, Ala., 1963.

16 HAMER, Marguerite B. "The Fate of the Exiled Acadians in South Carolina." *J S Hist,* IV (1938), 199-208.

17 HANLEY, Thomas O. "His Excellency's Council, Maryland, 1715-1720." *Rec Am Cath Hist Soc* LXXIV (1963), 137-150.

18 HEALY, Elliott D. "Acadian Exiles in Virginia." *Fr Rev,* XXII (1949), 233-240.

19 HERSHBERGER, Guy F. "Pacifism and the State in Colonial Pennsylvania." *Ch Hist,* VIII (1939), 54-74.

20 HINDLE, Brooke. "The March of the Paxton Boys." *Wm Mar Q,* 3rd ser., III (1946), 461-486.

21 HUDNUT, Ruth A. and Hayes BAKER-CROTHERS. "Acadian Transients in South Carolina." *Am Hist Rev,* XLII (1938), 500-513.

22 KAMMEN, Michael G. "The Causes of the Maryland Revolution of 1689." *Md Hist Mag,* LV (1960), 293-333.

1 KEMMERER, Donald L. "Judges' Good Behavior Tenure in Colonial New Jersey." *Proc N J Hist Soc,* LVI (1938), 18-30.

2 KETCHAM, Ralph L. "Benjamin Franklin and William Smith: New Light on an Old Philadelphia Quarrel." *Pa Mag Hist,* LXXXVIII (1964), 142-163.

3 KETCHAM, Ralph L. "Conscience, War, and Politics in Pennsylvania, 1755-1757." *Wm Mar Q,* 3rd ser., XX (1963), 416-439.

4 KLEIN, Milton M. "Prelude to Revolution in New York: Jury Trials and Judicial Tenure." *Wm Mar Q,* 3rd ser., XVII (1960), 439-462.

5 LEAMON, James S. "Governor Fletcher's Recall." *Wm Mar Q,* 3rd ser., XV (1963), 527-542.

6 LEDER, Lawrence H. "The Glorious Revolution and the Pattern of Imperial Relationships." *N Y Hist,* XLVI (1965), 203-212.

7 LEDER, Lawrence H. "The Politics of Upheaval in New York, 1689-1709." *N-Y Hist Soc Q,* XLIV (1960), 413-427.

8 LEDER, Lawrence H. "Robert Livingston: A New View of New York Politics." *N Y Hist,* XL (1959), 358-367.

9 LEFLER, Hugh T. and Paul WAGER, eds. *Orange County–1752-1952.* Chapel Hill, 1952.

10 LONDON, Lawrence F. "The Representation Controversy in Colonial North Carolina." *N C Hist Rev,* XI (1934), 255-270.

11 MC CORMAC, Eugene I. *Colonial Opposition to Imperial Authority During the French and Indian War.* Berkeley, 1911.

12 MC GUIRE, Maureen. "Struggle over the Purse: Governor Morris versus the New Jersey Assembly." *Proc N J Hist Soc,* LXXXII (1964), 200-207.

13 MASON, Bernard. "Aspects of the New York Revolt of 1689." *N Y Hist,* XXX (1949), 165-180.

14 MATTHEWS, Albert. "Acceptance of the Explanatory Charter, 1725-1726." *Pub Col Soc Mass,* XIV (1913), 389-400.

15 MORRIS, Richard B. "Spotlight on the Plowmen of the Jersies." *Proc N J Hist Soc,* LXVII (1949), 106-123.

16 NASH, Gary B. "The Free Society of Traders and the Early Politics of Pennsylvania." *Pa Mag Hist,* LXXXIX (1965), 147-173.

17 OWINGS, Donnell M. *His Lordship's Patronage: Offices of Profit in Colonial Maryland.* Baltimore, 1953.

18 REICH, Jerome R. *Leisler's Rebellion: A Study of Democracy in New York, 1664-1720.* Chicago, 1953.

19 ROTHERMUND, Dietmar. "The German Problem of Colonial Pennsylvania." *Pa Mag Hist,* LXXXIV (1960), 3-21.

20 ROTHERMUND, Dietmar. "Political Factions and the Great Awakening." *Pa Hist,* XXVI (1959), 317-331.

21 SCHUTZ, John A. "Succession Politics in Massachusetts, 1730-1741." *Wm Mar Q,* 3rd ser., XV (1958), 508-520.

22 SCOTT, Arthur P. "The Constitutional Aspects of the 'Parson's Cause'." *Pol Sci Q,* XXXI (1916), 558-577.

23 SCOTT, Kenneth. "'Rattling' Verses on Royal Prerogative." *N Y Fklr Q,* XIII (1957), 195-203.

1 SHY, John. "Quartering His Majesty's Forces in New Jersey." *Proc N J Hist Soc,* LXXVIII (1960), 82-94.

2 SIOUSSAT, St. George L. *The English Statutes in Maryland.* Baltimore, 1903.

3 SIRMANS, M. Eugene. "The South Carolina Royal Council, 1720-1763." *Wm Mar Q,* 3rd ser., XVIII (1961), 373-392.

4 SKLAR, Robert. "The Great Awakening and Colonial Politics: Connecticut's Revolution in the Minds of Men." *Bull Conn Hist Soc,* XXVIII (1963), 81-95.

5 SPENCER, Charles W. "Sectional Aspects of New York Provincial Politics." *Pol Sci Q,* XXX (1915), 397 424.

6 SYDNOR, Charles S. *Political Leadership in Eighteenth Century Virginia.* Oxford, 1951.

7 TAYLOR, Paul. "Colonizing Georgia, 1732-1752: A Statistical Note." *Wm Mar Q,* XXII (1965), 119-127.

8 THOMPSON, Mack E. "The Ward-Hopkins Controversy and the American Revolution in Rhode Island: an Interpretation." *Wm Mar Q,* 3rd ser., XVI (1959), 363-375.

9 TOLLES, Frederick B., ed. "The Twilight of the Holy Experiment: A Contemporary View." *Bull Frnds Hist Assn,* XLV (1956), 30-37.

10 TURNER, Gordon B. "Governor Lewis Morris and the Colonial Government Conflict." *Proc N J Hist Soc,* LXVII (1949), 260-304.

11 WARDEN, G. B. "The Proprietary Group in Pennsylvania, 1754-1764." *Wm Mar Q,* 3rd ser., XXI (1964), 367-389.

12 WATERS, John J., Jr. and John A. SCHUTZ. "Patterns of Massachusetts Colonial Politics: The Writs of Assistance and the Rivalry between the Otis and Hutchinson Families." *Wm Mar Q,* 3rd ser., XXIV (1967), 543-567.

13 WENDEL, Thomas. "The Keith-Lloyd Alliance: Factional and Coalition Politics in Colonial Pennsylvania." *Pa Mag Hist,* XCII (1968), 289-305.

14 WRIGHT, Louis B. "William Byrd's Defense of Sir Edmund Andros." *Wm Mar Q,* 3rd ser., II (1945), 47-62.

15 WRIGHT, Louis B. "William Byrd's Opposition to Governor Francis Nicholson." *J S Hist,* XI (1945), 68-79.

16 ZIMMERMAN, John J. "Benjamin Franklin and the 'Heads of Complaints.'" *Pa Mag Hist,* LXXXV (1961), 75-77.

17 ZIMMERMAN, John J. "Benjamin Franklin and the Quaker Party, 1755-1756." *Wm Mar Q,* 3rd ser., XVII (1960), 291-313.

18 ZIMMERMAN, John J. "Governor Denny and the Quartering Act of 1756." *Pa Mag Hist,* XCI (1967), 266-281.

Intercolonial Rivalries

19 FOX, Dixon Ryan. *Yankees and Yorkers.* New York, 1940.

20 JOHANNSEN, Robert W. "The Conflict Between the Three Lower Counties on the Delaware and the Province of Pennsylvania, 1682-1704." *Del Hist,* V (1952), 96-132.

21 NASH, Gary B. "Maryland's Economic War with Pennsylvania." *Md Hist Mag,* LX (1965), 231-243.

1 POWELL, Walter A. "Fight of a Century between the Penns and Calverts." *Md Hist Mag,* XXIX (1934), 83-101.

2 SKAGGS, Marvin L. "Progress in the North Carolina-South Carolina Boundary Dispute." *N C Hist Rev,* XV (1938), 341-353.

3 SMITH, Jonathan. "The Massachusetts and New Hampshire Boundary Line Controversy, 1693-1740." *Proc Mass Hist Soc,* XLIII (1910), 77-88.

Military and Indian Affairs

4 AMBLER, Charles H. *George Washington and the West.* Chapel Hill, 1936.

5 BAILEY, Kenneth P. *Thomas Cresap, Maryland Frontiersman..* Boston, 1944.

6 BAKER-CROTHERS, Hayes. *Virginia and the French and Indian War.* Chicago, 1928.

7 BUFFINTON, Arthur H. "Governor Dudley and the Proposed Treaty of Neutrality, 1705." *Pub Col Soc Mass,* XXVI (1927), 211-229.

8 CRANE, Verner W. *The Southern Frontier.* See 18.17.

9 EVERETT, Edward G. "Pennsylvania's Indian Diplomacy, 1747-1753." *W Pa Hist Mag,* XLIV (1961), 241-256.

10 GIDDENS, Paul H. "The French and Indian War in Maryland, 1753 to 1756." *Md Hist Mag,* XXX (1934), 281-310.

11 GRAEFE, Arthur D. *Conrad Weiser, Pennsylvania Peacemaker.* Fogelsville, Pa., 1945.

12 GRIFFITH, Lucille. "South Carolina and Fort Alabama, 1714-1763." *Ala Rev,* XII (1959), 258-271.

13 HUNTER, William A. *Forts on the Pennsylvania Frontier, 1753-1758.* Harrisburg, Pa., 1960.

14 JONES, E. Alfred. "The American Regiment in the Carthagena Expedition." *Va Mag Hist,* XXX (1922), 1-20.

15 KOONTZ, Louis K. *The Virginia Frontier, 1754-1763.* Baltimore, 1925.

16 LABAREE, Leonard W. "Benjamin Franklin and the Defense of Pennsylvania, 1754-1757." *Pa Hist,* XXIX (1962), 7-23.

17 LANNING, John T. "The American Colonies in the Preliminaries of the War of Jenkins' Ear." *Ga Hist Q,* XI (1927), 129-155.

18 LANNING, John T. "American Participation in the War of Jenkins' Ear." *Ga Hist Q,* XI (1927), 191-215.

19 LEACH, Douglas E. *The Northern Colonial Frontier.* See 19.8.

20 MOORE, Howard P. *A Life of General John Stark of New Hampshire.* New York, 1949.

21 NIXON, Lily L. *James Burd, Frontier Defender, 1726-1793.* Philadelphia, 1941.

22 SCHLESINGER, Arthur M. "Maryland's Share in the Last Intercolonial War." *Md Hist Mag,* VII (1912), 119-149, 243-268.

23 TRIMBLE, David B. "Christopher Gist and the Indian Service in Virginia, 1757-1759." *Va Mag Hist,* LXIV (1956), 143-165.

1 VOLWILER, Albert T. *George Croghan and the Westward Movement, 1741-1782.* Cleveland, 1926.

2 WAINWRIGHT, Nicholas B. *George Croghan: Wilderness Diplomat.* Chapel Hill, 1959.

3 WALLACE, Paul A. W. *Conrad Weiser, 1696-1760: Friend of Colonist and Mohawk.* Philadelphia, 1945.

4 WALLER, G. M. "New York's Role in Queen Anne's War, 1702-1713." *N Y Hist,* XXXIII (1952), 40-53.

Economic and Social Development

GENERAL

5 BRIDENBAUGH, Carl. *Myths and Realities: Societies of the Colonial South.* New York, 1963.†

6 BRUCHEY, Stuart. *The Roots of American Economic Growth, 1607-1861.* New York, 1965.†

7 *Historical Statistics of the United States, Colonial Times to 1957.* Washington, D.C., 1960.

8 KNAUSS, James O. *Social Conditions among the Pennsylvania Germans in the Eighteenth Century, as Revealed in German Newspapers published in America.* Lancaster, Pa., 1922.

9 MERRENS, H. Roy. "Historical Geography and Early American History." See **25**.19.

10 SACHS, William S. and Ari HOOGENBOOM. *The Enterprising Colonials: Society on the Eve of the Revolution.* Chicago, 1965.

11 SHIPTON, Clifford K. *New England Life in the 18th Century. Representative Biographies from Sibley's Harvard Graduates.* Cambridge, Mass., 1963.

12 SUTHERLAND, Stella H. "Colonial Statistics." *Explor Entrep Hist,* V (1967), 58-107.

13 TAYLOR, George R. "American Economic Growth before 1840: An Exploratory Essay." *J Econ Hist,* XXIV (1964), 427-444.

14 WEEDEN, William B. *Economic and Social History of New England, 1620 1789.* 2 vols. Boston, 1890.

DEMOGRAPHY

General

15 ALDRIDGE, Alfred O. "Franklin as Demographer." *J Econ Hist,* IX (1949), 25-44.

16 DUNAWAY, Wayland F. "Pennsylvania as an Early Distributing Center of Population." *Pa Mag Hist,* LV (1931), 134-169.

17 FRIIS, Herman R. *A Series of Population Maps of the Colonies and the United States, 1625-1790.* New York, 1940.

18 GREENE, Evarts B. and Virginia D. HARRINGTON. *American Population before the Federal Census of 1790.* New York, 1932.

1 MOOD, Fulmer. "Studies in the History of American Settled Areas and Frontier Lines . . . 1625-1790." *Ag Hist,* XXVI (1952), 16-34.

2 POTTER, J. "The Growth of Population in America, 1700-1860," *Population in History, Essays in Historical Demography,* ed. D. V. Glass and D. E. C. Eversley. Chicago, 1965.

3 ROSSITER, W. S. *A Century of Population Growth.* Washington, D. C., 1909.

4 SUTHERLAND, Stella H. *Population Distribution in Colonial America.* New York, 1936.

5 THOMPSON, Warren S. "The Demographic Revolution in the United States." *Ann Am Acad Pol Sci,* no. 262 (1949), 62-69.

6 WHITNEY, Herbert A. "Estimating Precensus Populations: A Method Suggested and Applied to the Towns of Rhode Island and Plymouth Colonies in 1689." *Ann Assn Am Geog,* LV (1965), 179-189.

Studies of Individual Colonies

7 BRUSH, John E. *The Population of New Jersey.* New Brunswick, N. J., 1956.

8 DEMOS, John "Families in Colonial Bristol, Rhode Island: An Exercise in Historical Demography." *Wm Mar Q,* 3rd ser., XXV (1968), 40-57.

9 FELT, Joseph B. "Statistics of Towns in Massachusetts" and "Statistics of Population in Massachusetts." *Coll Am Statis Assn,* I (1847).

10 KARINEN, Arthur E. "Maryland Population, 1631-1730: Numerical and Distributive Aspects." *Md Hist Mag,* LIV (1959), 365-407.

11 KARINEN, Arthur E. "Numerical and Distributional Aspects of Maryland Population, 1631-1840." *Md Hist Mag,* LX (1965), 139-159.

12 LOCKRIDGE, Kenneth. "Land, Population and the Evolution of New England Society 1630-1790," *Past Pres,* no. 39 (1968), 62-80.

13 MERRENS, H. Roy. *Colonial North Carolina.* See **25**.9.

14 OLSON, Albert L. *Agricultural Economy and the Population in Eighteenth-Century Connecticut.* New Haven, 1935.

15 PETTY, Julian J. *The Growth and Distribution of Population in South Carolina.* Columbia, S. C., 1943.

Sex Distribution, Fertility, and Marriage Age

16 CRUM, Frederick S. "The Decadence of the Native American Stock: A Statistical Study of Genealogical Records." *Pub Am Stat Assn,* XIV (1914), 215-222.

17 JACOBUS, Donald L. "Age of Girls at Marriage in Colonial New England." *Am Geneal,* XXVII (1951), 116-118.

18 MOLLER, Herbert. "Sex Composition and Correlated Culture Patterns of Colonial America." *Wm Mar Q,* 3rd ser., II (1945), 113-153.

19 MONAHAN, Thomas P. *The Pattern of Age at Marriage in the United States.* 2 vols. Philadelphia, 1951.

IMMIGRATION
See the section on Labor for additional listings.

General

1 BUTTERFIELD, Roy L. "On the American Migrations." *N Y Hist,* XXXVIII (1957), 368-386.

2 CORRY, John P. "Racial Elements in Colonial Georgia." *Ga Hist Q,* XX (1936), 30-40.

3 DUFFY, John. "The Passage to the Colonies." *Miss Val Hist Rev,* XXXVIII (1951), 21-38.

4 HANSEN, Marcus L. *The Atlantic Migration, 1607-1860: A History of the Continuing Settlement of the United States.* Cambridge, Mass., 1940.†

5 "Report of the Committee on Linguistic and National Stocks in the Population of the United States." *Am Hist Assn Ann Rep,* I (1932), 105-441.

6 RISCH, Erna. "Encouragement of Immigration as Revealed in Colonial Legislation." *Va Mag Hist,* XLV (1937), 1-10.

7 SHIPTON, Clifford K. "Immigration to New England, 1680-1740." *J Pol Econ,* XLIV (1936), 225-239.

8 WITTKE, Carl. *We Who Built America: The Saga of the Immigrant.* New York, 1939.†

English Immigration

9 CAMPBELL, Mildred. "English Emigration on the Eve of the American Revolution." *Am Hist Rev,* LXI (1955), 1-20.

10 THOMAS, John P., Jr. "The Barbadians in Early South Carolina." *S C Hist Mag* XXXI (1930), 75-92.

The French Huguenots

11 BAIRD, George W. *History of the Huguenot Emigration to America.* 2 vols. New York, 1885.

12 CHINARD, Gilbert. *Réfugiés Huguenots en Amérique, avec une Introduction sur le Mirage Américain.* Paris, 1925.

13 DOUGLAS, Donald. *The Huguenot; The Story of the Huguenot Emigrations, Particularly to New England.* New York, 1954.

14 DUCLOS, R. P. *Histoire du Protestantisme Français au Canada et aux Etats-Unis.* 2 vols. Lausanne, 1913.

15 HIRSCH, Arthur H. *The Huguenots of Colonial South Carolina.* Durham, N. C., 1928.

16 LAUX, J. B. *The Huguenot Element in Pennsylvania.* New York, 1896.

17 WEISS, Charles. *History of the French Protestant Refugees from the Revocation of the Edict of Nantes to our own Days.* 2 vols. New York, 1854.

The Scots

General

18 DICKSON, R. J. *Ulster Emigration to Colonial America 1718-1775.* London, 1966.

1 GRAHAM, Ian C. C. *Colonists from Scotland. Emigration to North America, 1707-1783.* Ithaca, 1956.

2 PRYDE, George S. "Scottish Colonization in the Province of New York." *N Y Hist,* XVI (1935), 138-157.

The Scotch Irish

3 DUNAWAY, Wayland F. *The Scotch-Irish of Colonial Pennsylvania.* Chapel Hill, 1944.

4 FORD, H. J. *The Scotch-Irish in America.* Princeton, 1915.

5 GREEN, Edward R. R. "Scotch-Irish Emigration, an Imperial Problem." *W Pa Hist Mag,* XXXV (1952), 193-209.

6 GREEN, Edward R. R. "The 'Strange Humors' that Drove the Scotch-Irish to America, 1729." *Wm Mar Q,* 3rd ser., XII (1955), 113-123.

7 HANNA, C. A. *The Scotch-Irish, or, the Scot in North Britain, North Ireland, and North America.* 2 vols. New York, 1902.

8 KLETT, Guy Soulliard. *The Scotch Irish in Pennsylvania.* Gettysburg, Pa., 1948.

9 LEYBURN, James G. *The Scotch-Irish: A Social History.* Chapel Hill, 1962.

The Highland Scots

10 MAC DONELL, Alexander R. "The Settlement of the Scotch Highlanders at Darien." *Ga Hist Q,* XX (1936), 250-262.

11 MEYER, Duane. *The Highland Scots of North Carolina, 1732-1776.* Chapel Hill, 1961.

The Germans

12 BOLZIUS, Johann Martin. "Johan Martin Bolzius Answers a Questionnaire on Carolina and Georgia." Trans. and ed. Klaus G. Leowald, Beverly Starika, and Paul S. Taylor. *Wm Mar Q,* 3rd ser., XIV (1957), 218-261.

13 CUNZ, Dieter. *The Maryland Germans: A History.* Princeton, 1948.

14 DIFFENDERFER, F. R. *The German Immigration into Pennsylvania through the Port of Philadelphia: 1700 to 1775.* Lancaster, Pa., 1900.

15 DORPALEN, Andreas. "The Political Influence of the German Element in Colonial America." *Pa Hist,* VI (1939), 147-158, 221-239.

16 FAUST, A. B. *The German Element in the United States.* 2 vols. New York, 1909.

17 FRIES, Adelaide L. "The Moravian Contribution to Colonial North Carolina." *N C Hist Rev,* VII (1930), 1-14.

18 HOFER, J. M. "The Georgia Salzburgers." *Ga Hist Q,* XVIII (1934), 99-117.

19 HOLDER, Edward M. "Social Life of the Early Moravians in North Carolina." *N C Hist Rev* XI (1934), 167-184.

20 JOHNSON, William T. "Some Aspects of the Relations of the Government and German Settlers in Colonial Pennsylvania, 1683-1754." *Pa Hist,* (1944), 81-102, 200-207.

1   JORDAN, John W. "Moravian Immigration to Pennsylvania, 1734-1765." *Pa Mag Hist,* XXXIII (1909), 228-248.

2   KLEES, Frederic. *The Pennsylvania Dutch.* New York, 1950.

3   KNITTLE, W. A. *The Early Eighteenth Century Palatine Emigration.* Philadelphia, 1936.

4   KREBS, Frederick, Comp. *Emigrants from the Palatinate to the American Colonies in the 18th Century.* Norristown, Pa., 1953.

5   KUHNS, Levi O. *The German and Swiss Settlements of Colonial Pennsylvania.* New York, 1901.

6   NEWTON, Hester W. "The Industrial and Social Influences of the Salzburgers in Colonial Georgia." *Ga Hist Q,* XVIII (1934), 335-353.

7   POCHMANN, Henry A. *German Culture in America. Philosophical and Literary Influences. 1600-1900.* Madison, Wis., 1957.

8   POLLAK, Otto. "German Immigrant Problems in Eighteenth Century Pennsylvania as Reflected in Trouble Advertisements." *Am Socio Rev,* VIII (1943), 674-684.

9   ROBERTS, Charles R. "Pennsylvania Germans in Public Life during the Colonial Period." *Pa-Ger,* X (1909), 153-157.

10   SCHULTZ, Selina G. "The Schwenkfelders of Pennsylvania." *Pa Hist,* XXIV (1957), 293-321.

11   SMITH, C. Henry. *The Mennonite Immigration to Pennsylvania in the Eighteenth Century.* Norristown, Pa., 1929.

12   WALLACE, Paul A. W. *The Muhlenbergs of Pennsylvania.* Philadelphia, 1950.

13   WOLTERS, Richard. "An Eighteenth-Century Account of German Emigration to the American Colonies." Ed. Frank Spencer. *J Mod Hist,* XXVIII (1956), 55-59.

14   WOOD, Ralph, ed. *Pennsylvania Germans* Princeton, 1942.

Jews

15   ADELMAN, David C. "Strangers. Civil Rights of Jews in the Colony of Rhode Island." *R I Jew Hist Note,* I (1954), 104-118.

16   BETHENCOURT, Cardoza de. "Notes on the Spanish and Portuguese Jews in the United States, Guiana, and the Dutch and British West Indies during the Seventeenth and Eighteenth Centuries." *Am Jew Hist Soc Pub,* XXIX (1925), 7-38.

17   BROCHES, S. *Jews in New England.* 2 vols. New York, 1942.

18   ELZAS, Barnett A. *The Jews of South Carolina.* Philadelphia, 1905.

19   FRIEDMAN, Lee M. *Early American Jews.* Cambridge, Mass., 1934.

20   FRIEDMAN, Lee M. "Jews in Early American Literature." *More Books,* XVII (1942), 455-474.

21   GOODMAN, Abram V. *American Overture: Jewish Rights in Colonial Times.* Philadelphia, 1947.

22   GRINSTEIN, Hyman B. *The Rise of the Jewish Community of New York, 1654-1860.* Philadelphia, 1945.

1 HUHNER, Leon. "Jews in the Legal and Medical Professions in America prior to 1800." *Am Jew Hist Soc Pub,* XXII (1914), 147-165.

2 MARCUS, Jacob R. *American Jewry: Documents, Eighteenth Century.* Cincinnati, 1959.

3 MARCUS, Jacob R. *Early American Jewry.* 2 vols. Philadelphia, 1951-1953.

4 PFEIFFER, Robert H. "The Teaching of Hebrew in Colonial America." *Jew Q Rev,* XLV (1955), 363-373.

5 POOL, D. de Sola. "Hebrew Learning Among the Puritans of New England prior to 1700." *Am Jew Hist Soc Pub,* XX (1911), 31-83.

6 REZNIKOFF, Charles. "Boston's Jewish Community. Earlier Days." *Commentary,* XV (1953), 490-499.

7 REZNIKOFF, Charles. "Manhattan's Oldest Jewish Settlers. The Sephardi Grandees Suffer a Sea Change." *Commentary,* XV (1953), 74-77.

8 RISCH, Erna. "Joseph Crellius, Immigrant Broker." *N Eng Q,* XII (1939), 241-267.

9 ROSENBLOOM, Joseph R. *A Biographical Dictionary of Early American Jews, Colonial Times through 1800.* Lexington, Ky., 1960.

10 WOLF, Edwin, II and Maxwell WHITEMAN. *The History of the Jews of Philadelphia from Colonial Times to the Age of Jackson.* Philadelphia, 1957.

Africans

11 CANTOR, Milton. "The Image of the Negro in Colonial Literature." *N Eng Q,* XXXVI (1963), 452-477.

12 GREENE, Lorenzo J. *The Negro in Colonial New England, 1620-1776.* New York, 1942.

13 HURWITZ, Samuel J. and Edith F. "A Token of Freedom: Private Bill Legislation for Free Negroes in Eighteenth-Century Jamaica," *Wm Mar Q,* 3rd ser., XXIV (1967), 423-431.

14 PORTER, Kenneth W. "Negroes on the Southern Frontier, 1670-1763." *J Neg Hist,* XXXIII (1948), 53-78.

15 READ, Allen W. "Speech Defects and Mannerisms among Slaves and Servants in Colonial America." *Q J Sp,* XXIV (1938), 397-401.

16 READ, Allen W. "The Speech of Negroes in Colonial America." *J Neg Hist,* XXIV (1939), 247-258.

17 RUSSELL, John H. *The Free Negro in Virginia, 1619-1865.* Baltimore, 1913.

18 TATE, Thad W. *The Negro in Eighteenth Century Williamsburg.* Williamsburg, Va., 1965.

19 WRIGHT, James M. *The Free Negro in Maryland, 1634-1860.* New York, 1921.

Other Groups

Swiss

20 FAUST, Albert B. "Swiss Emigration to the American Colonies in the Eighteenth Century." *Am Hist Rev,* XXII (1916), 21-44.

Dutch

21 HULL, William I. *William Penn and the Dutch Quaker Migration to Pennsylvania.* Swarthmore, 1935.

Irish

1 DONOVAN, George F. *The Pre-Revolutionary Irish in Massachusetts, 1620-1775.* Menasha, Wis., 1932.

2 MYERS, Albert C. *Immigration of the Irish Quakers into Pennsylvania, 1682-1750. With their Early History in Ireland . . . .* Swarthmore, 1902.

3 PURCELL, Richard J. "Irish Builders of Colonial Rhode Island." *Stud,* XXIV (1935), 289-300.

4 PURCELL, Richard J. "Irish Colonists in Colonial Maryland." *Stud,* XXIII (1934), 279-294.

5 PURCELL, Richard J. "Irish Contribution to Colonial New York." *Stud,* XXIX (1940), 591-604.

Italians

6 MARRARO, Howard R. "Italo-Americans in Eighteenth Century New York." *N Y Hist,* XXI (1940), 316-323.

7 MARRARO, Howard R. "Italo-Americans in Pennsylvania in the Eighteenth Century." *Pa Hist,* VII (1940), 159-166.

Naturalization and Assimilation

8 CARPENTER, A. H. "Naturalization in England and the American Colonies." *Am Hist Rev,* IX (1904), 288-304.

9 HOYT, Edward A. "Naturalization under the American Colonies: Signs of a New Community." *Pol Sci Q,* LXVII (1952), 248-266.

10 READ, Allen W. "The Assimilation of the Speech of British Immigrants in Colonial America." *J Eng Ger Philol,* XXXVII (1938), 70-79.

11 READ, Allen W. "Bilingualism in the Middle Colonies, 1725-1775." *Am Sp* XII (1937), 93-99.

12 START, Cora. "Naturalization in the English Colonies of America." *Am Hist Assn Ann Rep,* 1893 (1894), 317-338.

URBANIZATION

General

13 BRIDENBAUGH, Carl. *Cities in Revolt: Urban Life in America, 1743-1776.* New York, 1955.†

14 BRIDENBAUGH, Carl. *Cities in the Wilderness: The First Century of Urban Life in America, 1625-1742.* New York, 1938.†

15 BRIDENBAUGH, Carl. "The New England Town: A Way of Life." *Proc Am Ant Soc,* LVI (1946), 19-48.

Studies of Individual Towns

16 DILL, Alonzo T., Jr. "Eighteenth Century New Bern: A History of the Town and Craven County, 1700-1800." *N C Hist Rev,* XXIII (1946), 47-78.

17 GOULD, Clarence P. "The Economic Causes of the Rise of Baltimore." *Essays in Colonial History Presented to Charles McLean Andrews by his Students.* New Haven, 1931.

18 KIMBALL, Gertrude S. *Providence in Colonial Times.* Boston, 1912.

1 LEE, E. Lawrence. "Old Brunswick: The Story of a Colonial Town." *N C Hist Rev,* XXIX (1952), 230-245.

2 LEMON, James T. "Urbanization and the Development of Eighteenth-Century Southeastern Pennsylvania and Adjacent Delaware." *Wm Mar Q,* 3rd ser., XXIV (1967), 501-542.

3 PHILLIPS, James D. *Salem in the Eighteenth Century.* Boston, 1937.

4 RILEY, Edward M. "Suburban Development of Yorktown, Virginia, during the Colonial Period." *Va Mag Hist,* LX (1952), 522-536.

5 RILEY, Edward M. "The Town Acts of Colonial. Virginia." *J S Hist,* XVI (1950), 306-323.

6 ROSS, Marjorie D. *The Book of Boston: The Colonial Period, 1630-1775.* New York, 1960.

7 SALTONSTALL, William G. *Ports of Piscataqua.* Cambridge, Mass., 1941.

8 SOLTOW, James H. *The Economic Role of Williamsburg.* Williamsburg, Va., 1965.

9 WEEDEN, William B. "Early Commercial Providence." *Proc Am Ant Soc,* XIX (1909), 420-429.

10 WELSH, Peter C. "Merchants, Millers and Ocean Ships: The Components of an Early American Industrial Town." *Del Hist,* VII (1957), 319-336.

THE STRUCTURE OF OPPORTUNITY: THE LAND

Weather and Soils

11 HIGBEE, Edward C. "The Three Earths of New England." *Geog Rev,* XLII (1952), 425-438.

12 LUDLUM, David M. *Early American Hurricanes, 1492-1870,* Boston, 1963.

13 LUDLUM, David M. *Early American Winters, 1604-1820.* Boston, 1966.

14 MORRIS, F. G. "Environment and Regional Development in the Colonial Period." *Soc Forces,* XVI (1937), 12-23.

15 SAUER, Carl O. "The Settlement of the Humid East." In *Climate and Man* (U.S. Dept. Agric. Year Book, 1941). Washington, D.C., 1941.

The Process of Settlement

16 CARUSO, John A. *The Appalachian Frontier: America's First Surge Westward.* New York, 1959.

17 DODGE, Stanley D. "The Frontier of New England in the Seventeenth and Eighteenth Centuries and its Significance in American History" *Pap Mich Acad,* XXVIII (1942), 435-439.

18 HIGGINS, Ruth L. *Expansion in New York, With Especial Reference to the Eighteenth Century.* Columbus, Ohio, 1931.

19 MATHEWS, Lois K. *The Expansion of New England, the Spread of New England Settlement and Institutions to the Mississippi River, 1620-1865.* Boston, 1909.

20 MERIWETHER, Robert L. *The Expansion of South Carolina, 1729-1765.* Kingsport, Tenn., 1940.

1 MORRIS, F. Grave. "Some Aspects of the Rural Settlement of New England in Colonial Times," in *London Essays in Geography,* ed. Laurence D. Stamp. Cambridge, Mass., 1951.

2 NIDDRIE, David L. "An Attempt at Planned Settlement in St. Kitts in the Early Eighteenth Century," *Carib Stud,* V (1966), no.4, 3-11.

3 PITMAN, Frank Wesley. "The Settlement and Financing of British West India Plantations in the Eighteenth Century," in *Essays in Colonial History Presented to Charles McLean Andrews.* . . . New Haven, 1931.

4 SCOFIELD, Edna. "The Origin of Settlement Patterns in Rural New England." *Geog Rev,* XXVIII (1938), 652-663.

5 ZELINSKY, Wilbur. "An Isochronic Map of Georgia Settlement, 1750-1850." *Geog Hist Q,* XXXV (1951), 191-195.

Land Systems

6 BOND, Beverly W. *The Quit-Rent System.* . . . See **31**.2.

7 CLARK, Franklin C. "The Commonage System of Rhode Island." *Mag Hist,* III (1906), 341-356; IV (1906), 17-25.

8 ENO, Joel N. "The English Manors in New York." *J Am Hist,* XVI (1922), 361-377.

9 FORD, Amelia C. *Colonial Precedents of Our National Land System as it Existed in 1800.* Madison, Wis., 1910.

10 GIDDENS, Paul H. "Land Policies and Administration in Colonial Maryland, 1753-1769." *Md Hist Mag,* XXVIII (1933), 142-171.

11 GOULD, Clarence P. *The Land System in Maryland, 1720-1765.* Baltimore, 1913.

12 HARRIS, Marshall D. *Origin of the Land Tenure System in the United States.* Ames, Iowa, 1953.

13 MARK, Irving. *Agrarian Conflicts in Colonial New York, 1711-1775.* New York, 1940.

14 MEAD, Nelson P. "Land System of the Connecticut Towns." *Pol Sci Q,* XXI (1906), 59-76.

15 MORGAN, Lawrence N. "Land Tenure in Proprietary North Carolina." *James Sprunt Hist Stud,* XII (1912), 41-63.

16 NEWMAN, Harry W. *Seignory in Early Maryland, with a List of Manors and Manor Lords.* Washington, D.C., 1949.

17 POMFRET, John E. "The First Purchasers of Pennsylvania, 1681-1700." *Pa Mag Hist,* LXXX (1956), 137-163.

18 SAKOLSKI, Aaron M. *Land Tenure and Land Taxation in America.* New York, 1957.

19 SCISCO, L. D. "The Plantation Type of Colony." *Am Hist Rev,* VIII (1903), 260-270.

20 SPENCER, Charles W. "The Land System of Colonial New York." *Proc N Y St Hist Assn,* XVI (1917), 150-164.

21 SUTHERLAND, Arthur E. "The Tenantry on the New York Manor." *Cornell Law Q,* XLI (1956), 620-639.

22 WYCKOFF, V. J. "The Sizes of Plantations in Seventeenth-Century Maryland." *Md Hist Mag,* XXXII (1937), 331-339.

Agriculture

General

1 BIDWELL, Percy W. and John I. FALCONER. *History of Agriculture in the Northern United States, 1620-1860.* Washington, D.C., 1925.

2 CARRIER, Lyman. *The Beginnings of Agriculture in America.* New York, 1923.

3 GRAY, Lewis C. *History of Agriculture in the Southern United States to 1860.* 2 vols. Washington, D.C., 1933.

4 SCHAFER, Joseph. *The Social History of American Agriculture.* New York, 1936.

Practices and Problems

5 *American Husbandry.* Ed. Harry J. Carman. New York, 1939.

6 BRAND, Donald D. "The Origin and Early Distribution of New World Cultivated Plants." *Ag Hist,* XIII (1939), 109-117.

7 BRESSLER, Leo A. "Agriculture among the Germans in Pennsylvania during the Eighteenth Century." *Pa Hist,* XXII (1955), 102-133.

8 COLEMAN, Kenneth, ed. "Agricultural Practices in Georgia's First Decade," by Hector Beringer de Beaufain. *Ag Hist,* XXXIII (1959), 196-199.

9 CRAVEN, Avery O. *Soil Exhaustion as a Factor in the Agricultural History of Virginia and Maryland, 1606-1860.* Urbana, Ill., 1926.

10 DOAR, David *Rice and Rice Planting in the South Carolina Low Country.* Charleston, S.C., 1936.

11 DUNBAR, Gary S. "Colonial Carolina Cowpens." *Ag Hist,* XXXV (1961), 125-131.

12 ELIOT, Jared. *Essays upon Field Husbandry in New England, and Other Papers, 1748-1762.* Ed. Harry J. Carman and Rexford G. Tugwell. New York, 1935.

13 FLETCHER, Stevenson W. *Pennsylvania Agriculture and Country Life, 1640-1840.* Harrisburg, Pa., 1950.

14 FLETCHER, Stevenson W. "The Subsistence Farming Period in Pennsylvania Agriculture, 1640-1840." *Pa Hist,* XIV (1947), 185-195.

15 FRANKLIN, W. Niel. "Agriculture in Colonial North Carolina." *N C Hist Rev,* III (1926), 539-574.

16 GAGLIARDO, John G. "Germans and Agriculture in Colonial Pennsylvania." *Pa Mag Hist,* LXXXIII (1959), 192-218.

17 HAYWOOD, C. Robert. "Mercantilism and South Carolina Agriculture, 1700-1763," *S C Hist Mag,* LX (1959), 15-27.

18 HERNDON, G. Melvin. "Hemp in Colonial Virginia." *Ag Hist,* XXXVII (1963), 86-93.

19 HERNDON, G. Melvin. "Indian Agriculture in the Southern Colonies." *N C Hist Rev.* XLIV (1967), 283-298.

20 HEYWARD, Duncan C. *Seed from Madagascar.* Chapel Hill, 1937.

21 LEMON, James T. "The Agricultural Practices of National Groups in Eighteenth Century Southeastern Pennsylvania." *Geog Rev,* LVI (1966) 467-496.

22 LOEHR, Rodney C. "Self-Sufficiency on the Farm." *Ag Hist,* XXVI (1952), 37-42.

1 MAIRS, Thomas I. *Some Pennsylvania Pioneers in Agricultural Science.* State College, Pa., 1928.

2 MILLER, Frederick K. "The Farmer at Work in Colonial Pennsylvania." *Pa Hist,* III (1936), 115-123.

3 NEWTON, Hester W. "The Agricultural Activities of the Salzburgers in Colonial Georgia." *Ga Hist Q,* XVIII (1934), 248-263.

4 PARRY, John H. "Plantation and Provision Ground: A Historical Sketch of the Introduction of Food Crops into Jamaica." *Rev Hist Am,* XXXIX (1955), 1-20.

5 PHILLIPS, Deane. *Horse Raising in Colonial New England.* Ithaca, N.Y., 1922.

6 RANGE, Willard. "The Agricultural Revolution in Royal Georgia, 1752-1775." *Ag Hist,* XXI (1947), 250-255.

7 SACHS, William S. "Agricultural Conditions in the Northern Colonies before the Revolution." *J Econ Hist,* XIII (1953), 274-290.

8 SCOVILLE, Warren C. "Did Colonial Farmers 'Waste' Our Land?" *S Econ J,* XX (1953), 178-181.

9 SHRYOCK, Richard H. "British Versus German Traditions in Colonial Agriculture." *Miss Val Hist Rev,* XXVI (1939), 39-54.

10 STETSON, Sarah P. "The Traffic in Seeds and Plants from England's Colonies in North America." *Ag Hist,* XXIII (1949), 45-56.

11 WALCOTT, Robert. "Husbandry in Colonial New England." *N Eng Q,* IX (1936), 218-252.

12 WEISS, Roger W. "Mr. Scoville on Colonial Land Wastage." *S Econ J,* XXI (1954), 87-90.

13 WOODWARD, Carl R. *The Development of Agriculture in New Jersey, 1640-1880, a Monographic Study in Agricultural History.* New Brunswick, N.J., 1927.

Thought and Experimentation

14 BROWNE, C. A. "Some Historical Relations of Agriculture in the West Indies to that of the United States." *Ag Hist,* I (1927), 23-33

15 COLLINSON, Peter and John CUSTIS. "Brothers of the Spade: Correspondence of Peter Collinson, of London, and of John Custis, of Williamsburg, Virginia, 1734-1746." Ed. Earl G. Swem. *Proc Am Ant Soc,* LVIII (1948), 17-190.

16 HILLDRUP, Robert L. "A Campaign to Promote the Prosperity of Colonial Virginia." *Va Mag Hist,* LXVII (1959), 410-428.

17 HIRSCH, Arthur H. "French Influence on American Agriculture in the Colonial Period with Special Reference to Southern Provinces." *Ag Hist,* IV (1930), 1-9.

18 HOLLAND, James W. "The Beginning of Public Agricultural Experimentation in America: The Trustees' Garden in Georgia." *Ag Hist,* XII (1938), 271-298.

19 MC CORMICK, Richard P. "The Royal Society, the Grape, and New Jersey." *Proc N J Hist Soc,* LXXXI (1963), 75-84.

20 TRUE, Rodney H. "Beginnings of Agricultural Literature in America." *Ala Bull,* XIV (1920), 186-194.

1 TRUE, Rodney H. "Jared Eliot, Minister, Physician, Farmer." *Ag Hist,* II (1928), 185-212.

2 WOODWARD, Carl R. "Agricultural Legislation in Colonial New Jersey." *Ag Hist,* III (1929), 15-28.

3 WOODWARD, Carl R. *Ploughs and Politicks: Charles Read of New Jersey and his Notes on Agriculture, 1715-1774.* New Brunswick, N.J., 1941.

4 WYCKOFF, Vertrees J. *Tobacco Regulation in Colonial Maryland.* Baltimore, 1936.

Studies of Groups

5 HALL, Douglas. "Absentee Proprietorship in the British West Indies to about 1850." *Jam Hist Rev,* IV (1964), 15-35.

6 LAND, Aubrey C. "Economic Behavior in a Planting Society: The Eighteenth-Century Chesapeake." *J S Hist,* XXXIII (1967), 469-485.

7 MILLER, William D. "The Narragansett Planters." *Proc Am Ant Soc,* XLIII (1934), 49-115.

8 MORTON, Louis. *Robert Carter of Nomini Hall: A Virginia Tobacco Planter of the Eighteenth Century.* Princeton, 1941.†

9 MORTON, Louis. "Robert Wormeley Carter of Sabine Hall: Some Notes on the Life of a Virginia Planter." *J S Hist,* XII (1946), 345-365.

10 PARES, Richard. *Merchants and Planters.* New York, 1960.†

11 PITMAN, F. W. *The Development of the British West Indies, 1700-1763.* New Haven, 1917.

12 POTTER, David M., Jr. "The Rise of the Plantation System in Georgia." *Ga Hist Q,* XVI (1932), 114-135.

13 RAGATZ, Lowell J. *Absentee Land-Lordism in the British Caribbean, 1750-1833.* London, 1929.

14 SHERIDAN, Richard B. "Letters from a Sugar Plantation in Antigua, 1739-1758." *Ag Hist,* XXXI (1957), 3-23.

15 SHERIDAN, Richard B. "The Rise of a Colonial Gentry: A Case Study of Antigua, 1730-1775." *Econ Hist Rev,* XIII (1961), 342-357.

16 WERTENBAKER, Thomas J. *The Planters of Colonial Virginia.* Princeton, 1922.

Concepts of the Farmer

17 EISINGER, Chester E. "The Farmer in the Eighteenth Century Almanac." *Ag Hist,* XXVIII (1954), 107-112.

18 EISINGER, Chester E. "The Freehold Concept in Eighteenth-Century American Letters." *Wm Mar Q,* 3rd ser., IV (1947), 42-59.

19 EISINGER, Chester E. "Land and Loyalty: Literary Expressions of Agrarian Nationalism in the Seventeenth and Eighteenth Centuries." *Am Lit,* XXI (1949), 160-178.

Land Development

20 AKAGI, Roy H. *The Town Proprietors of the New England Colonies; A Study of their Development, Organization, Activities and Controversies, 1620-1770.* Philadelphia, 1924.

21 BAILEY, Kenneth P. *The Ohio Company of Virginia and the Westward Movement, 1748-1792.* Glendale, Calif., 1939.

1 BOYD, Julian P. *The Susquehannah Company: Connecticut's Experiment in Expansion.* New Haven, 1935.

2 BYRNE, Jacob H. "Henry William Stiegel's Land Holdings." *Pap Lanc Co Hist Soc,* XXXIX (1935), 9-20.

3 FOX, Edith M. *Land Speculation in the Mohawk Country.* Ithaca, 1949.

4 GATES, Paul W. "The Role of the Land Speculator in Western Development." *Pa Mag Hist,* LXVI (1942), 314-333.

5 GRANT, Charles S. "Land Speculation and the Settlement of Kent, 1738-1760." *N Eng Q,* XXVIII (1955), 51-71.

6 HARLEY, R. Bruce. "Dr. Charles Carroll—Land Speculator, 1730-1755." *Md Hist Mag,* XLVI (1951), 93-107.

7 JAMES, Alfred P. *The Ohio Company, its Inner History.* Pittsburgh, Pa., 1959.

8 LAND, Aubrey C. "A Land Speculator in the Opening of Western Maryland." *Md Hist Mag,* XLVIII (1953), 191-203.

9 MORISON, Samuel Eliot. "A Generation of Expansion and Inflation in Massachusetts History. 1713-1741," *Pub Col Soc Mass,* XIX (1916-1917), 271-272.

10 POMFRET, John E. *The New Jersey Proprietors and their Lands, 1664-1776.* Princeton, 1964.

11 SELLERS, Charles G., Jr. "Private Profits and British Colonial Policy: The Speculations of Henry McCulloh." *Wm Mar Q,* 3rd ser., VIII (1951), 535-551.

12 SMITH, Abbott E. "The Indentured Servant and Land Speculation in Seventeenth Century Maryland." *Am Hist Rev,* XL (1935), 467-472.

13 VOORHIS, Manning C. "Crown Versus Council in the Virginia Land Policy." *Wm Mar Q,* 3rd ser., III (1946), 499-514.

14 WOODARD, Florence M. *The Town Proprietors in Vermont: The New England Town Proprietorship in Decline.* New York, 1936.

THE STRUCTURE OF OPPORTUNITY: COMMERCE

General

15 ANDREWS, Charles M. "Colonial Commerce." *Am Hist Rev,* XX (1914), 43-63.

16 ANDREWS, John H. "Anglo-American Trade in the Early Eighteenth Century." *Geog Rev,* XLV (1955), 99-110.

17 FARNIE, D. A. "The Commercial Empire of the Atlantic, 1607-1783." *Econ Hist Rev,* XV (1962-1963), 205-218.

18 GOULD, Clarence P. "Trade between the Windward Islands and the Continental Colonies of the French Empire, 1683-1763," *Miss Val Hist Rev,* XXV (1938-1939), 473-490.

19 JOHNSON, Emory R., and others. *History of Domestic and Foreign Commerce of the United States.* 2 vols. Washington, D.C., 1915.

20 MAC INNES, Charles M. *A Gateway of Empire.* London, 1939.

21 NETTELS, Curtis P. "England and the Spanish-American Trade, 1680-1715," *J Mod Hist,* III (1931), 1-32.

Conditions of Commercial Life

1 BAILYN, Bernard. "Communications and Trade: The Atlantic in the Seventeenth Century." *J Econ Hist,* XIII (1953),378-387.

2 BAIRD, E. G. "Business Regulation in Colonial Massachusetts (1620-1780)." *Dakota Law Rev,* III (1931), 227-256.

3 BAXTER, W. T. "Accounting in Colonial America." In *Studies in the History of Accounting.* Ed. A. C. Littleton and B. S. Yamey. Homewood, Ill., 1956.

4 BERG, Harry D. "Economic Consequences of the French and Indian War for the Philadelphia Merchants." *Pa Hist,* XIII (1946), 185-193.

5 BERG, Harry D. "The Organization of Business in Colonial Philadelphia." *Pa Hist,* X (1943), 157-177.

6 BRUCHEY, Stuart. "Success and Failure Factors: American Merchants in Foreign Trade in the Eighteenth and Early Nineteenth Centuries." *Bus Hist Rev,* XXXII (1958), 272-292.

7 COLE, Arthur H. "The Tempo of Mercantile Life in Colonial America." *Bus Hist Rev,* XXXIII (1959), 277-299.

8 DAVIS, Joseph S. *Essays in the Earlier History of American Corporations.* 2 vols. Cambridge, Mass., 1917.

9 JENSEN, Arthur L. "The Inspection of Exports in Colonial Pennsylvania." *Pa Mag Hist,* LXXVIII (1954), 275-297.

10 SEYBOLT, Robert F., ed. "Trade Agreements in Colonial Boston." *N Eng Q,* II (1929), 307-309.

Character of Overseas Trade

General

11 BAILYN, Bernard and Lotte. *Massachusetts Shipping 1697-1714: A Statistical Study.* Cambridge, Mass., 1959.

12 BOWDEN, William H. "The Commerce of Marblehead, 1665-1775." *Essex Inst Hist Coll,* LXVIII (1932), 117-146; *Commerce of Rhode Island, 1726-1800. Vol. I, 1726-1774; Coll Mass Hist Soc,* 7th ser., IX (1914).

13 COULTER, Calvin B., Jr. "The Import Trade of Colonial Virginia." *Wm Mar Q,* 3rd ser., II (1945), 296-314.

14 CRITTENDEN, Charles C. *The Commerce of North Carolina, 1763-1789.* New Haven, 1936.

15 DOW, George F. "Shipping and Trade in Early New England." *Proc Mass Hist Soc,* LXIV (1932), 185-201.

16 GAYLE, Charles J. "The Nature and Volume of Exports from Charleston, 1724-1774." *Proc S C Hist Assn,* 1937 (1940), 25-33.

17 GIDDENS, Paul H. "Trade and Industry in Colonial Maryland, 1753-1769." *J Econ Bus Hist,* IV (1932), 512-538.

18 HANNA, Mary A. *Trade of the Delaware District before the Revolution.* Northhampton, Mass., 1917.

19 HOOKER, Roland M. *The Colonial Trade of Connecticut.* New Haven, 1936.

20 HUNTLEY, Francis C. "The Seaborne Trade of Virginia in Mid-Eighteenth Century: Port Hampton." *Va Mag Hist,* LIX (1951), 297-308.

1 JAMES, Francis G. "Irish Colonial Trade in the Eighteenth Century." *Wm Mar Q,* 3rd ser., XX (1963), 574-584.

2 JENSEN, Arthur L. *The Maritime Commerce of Colonial Philadelphia.* Madison, Wis., 1963.

3 LAWSON, Murray G. "The Boston Merchant Fleet of 1753." *Am Neptune,* IX (1949), 207-215.

4 LAWSON, Murray G. "The Routes of Boston's Trade, 1752-1765." *Pub Col Soc Mass,* XXXVIII (1959), 81-120.

5 LYDON, James G. "Fish and Flour for Gold: Southern Europe and the Colonial American Balance of Payments." *Bus Hist Rev,* XXXIX (1965), 171-183.

6 LYDON, James G. "Philadelphia's Commercial Expansion, 1720-1739." *Pa Mag Hist,* XCI (1967), 401-418.

7 MARTIN, Margaret E. *Merchants and Trade of the Connecticut River Valley, 1750-1820.* Northampton, Mass., 1929.

8 MORISON, Samuel Eliot. "The Commerce of Boston on the Eve of the American Revolution." *Proc Am Ant Soc,* XXXII (1922), 24-51.

9 MORRISS, Margaret S. *Colonial Trade of Maryland, 1689-1715.* Baltimore, 1914.

10 NETTELS, Curtis P. "England's Trade with New England and New York, 1685-1720." *Pub Col Soc Mass,* XXVIII (1930-1933), 322-350.

11 STOUGHTON, John A. *A Corner Stone of Colonial Commerce.* Boston, 1911.

12 WALTON, Gary M. "Sources of Productivity Change in American Colonial Shipping, 1675-1775." *Econ Hist Rev,* 2nd ser., XX (1967), 67-78.

13 WALTON, Gary M. "A Quantitative Study of American Colonial Shipping: A Summary." *J Econ Hist,* XXVI (1966), 595-598.

14 WALTON, Gary M. "A Measure of Productivity Change in American Colonial Shipping." *Econ Hist Rev,* 2nd ser., XXI (1968), 268-282.

15 WEAVER, Glenn. "Some Aspects of Early Eighteenth-Century Connecticut Trade." *Bull Conn Hist Soc,* XXII (1957), 23-31.

16 Writer's Program of the Works Progress Administration. *Boston Looks Seaward.* Boston, 1941.

Shipping and Navigation

17 MC CUSKER, John J. "Colonial Tonnage Measurement: Five Philadelphia Merchant Ships as a Sample." *J Econ Hist,* XXVII (1967), 82-91.

18 MC ELROY, John W. "Seafaring in Seventeenth-Century New England." *N Eng Q,* VIII (1935), 331-364.

19 ROBINSON, John and George F. DOW. *The Sailing Ships of New England, 1607-1907.* Westminister, Md., 1953.

20 SEMMES, Raphael. *Captains and Mariners of Early Maryland.* Baltimore, 1937.

21 WROTH, Lawrence C. "Some American Contributions to the Art of Navigation, 1519-1802." *Proc Mass Hist Soc,* LXVIII (1952), 72-112.

The Tobacco Trade

22 HEMPHILL, John M., II. "Freight Rates in the Maryland Tobacco Trade, 1705-1762." *Md Hist Mag,* LIV (1959), 36-60.

1 KELBAUGH, Paul R. "Tobacco Trade in Maryland, 1700-1725." *Md Hist Mag,* XXVI (1931), 1-33.

2 MAC INNES, C. M. *The Early English Tobacco Trade.* London, 1926.

3 MIDDLETON, Arthur P. *Tobacco Coast: A Maritime History of Chesapeake Bay in the Colonial Era. . . .* Ed. George C. Mason. Newport News, Va., 1953.

4 PRICE, Jacob M. "The Economic Growth of the Chesapeake and the European Market, 1697-1775." *J Econ Hist,* XXIV (1964), 496-511.

5 PRICE, Jacob M. "The French Farmers-General ·in the Chesapeake: The MacKercher-Huber Mission of 1737-1738." *Wm Mar Q,* 3rd ser., XIV (1957), 125-153.

6 PRICE, Jacob M. "The Rise of Glasgow in the Chesapeake Tobacco Trade, 1707-1775." *Wm Mar Q,* 3rd ser., XI (1954), 179-199.

7 PRICE, Jacob M. *The Tobacco Adventure to Russia: Enterprise, Politics, and Diplomacy in the Quest for a Northern Market for English Colonial Tobacco.* Philadelphia, 1961.

8 SOLTOW, J. H. "Scottish Traders in Virginia, 1750-1775." *Econ Hist Rev,* XII (1959), 83-98.

The Slave Trade

9 CURTIN, Philip D. "Epidemiology and the Slave Trade," *Pol Sci Q,* LXXXIII (1968), 190-216.

10 DONNAN, Elizabeth, ed. *Documents Illustrative of the History of the Slave Trade to America. . . .* 4 vols. Washington, D.C., 1930-1935.

11 DUIGNAN, Peter. *The United States and the African Slave Trade, 1614-1862.* Stanford, Calif., 1963.

12 HIGGINS, W. Robert. "Charles Town Merchants and Factors Dealing in the External Negro Trade, 1735-1775." *S C Hist Mag,* LXV (1964), 205-217.

13 POPE-HENNESSEY, James. *Sins of the Fathers: A Study of the Atlantic Slave Traders, 1441-1807.* New York, 1968.

14 RIDDELL, William R. "Pre-Revolutionary Pennsylvania and the Slave Trade." *Pa Mag Hist,* LII (1928), 1-28.

15 ROTTENBERG, Simon. "The Business of Slave Trading," *S Atl Q,* LXVI (1967), 409-423.

16 SCOTT, Kenneth. "George Scott: Slave Trader of New Port." *Am Neptune,* XII (1952), 222-228.

17 SHERIDAN, R. B. "The Commercial and Financial Organization of the British Slave Trade, 1750-1807." *Econ Hist Rev,* XI (1958), 249-263.

18 WAX, Darold D. "Negro Imports into Pennsylvania, 1720-1807," *Pa Hist,* XXXII (1965), 254-287.

19 WAX, Darold D. "A Philadelphia Surgeon on a Slaving Voyage to Africa, 1749-1751," *Pa Mag Hist,* XCII (1968), 465-493.

20 WAX, Darold D. "Quaker Merchants and the Slave Trade in Colonial Pennsylvania." *Pa Mag Hist,* LXXXVI (1962), 143-159.

21 WAX, Darold D. "Robert Ellis, Philadelphia Merchant and Slave Trader." *Pa Mag Hist,* LXXXVIII (1964), 52-69.

The Sugar Trade

1 ANDREWS, Charles M. "Anglo-French Commercial Rivalry, 1700-1750: The Western Phase." *Am Hist Rev,* XX (1915), 539-556, 761-780.

2 BELL, Herbert C. "The West India Trade before the Revolution." *Am Hist Rev,* XXII (1917), 272-287.

3 DAVIES, K. G. "The Origins of the Commission System in the West India Trade," *Roy Hist Soc Trans,* 5th ser., II (1952), 89-109.

4 HOULETTE, William D. "Rum-Trading in the American Colonies before 1763." *J Am Hist,* XXVIII (1934), 129-152.

5 OSTRANDER, Gilman M. "The Colonial Molasses Trade." *Ag Hist,* XXX (1956), 77-84.

6 PARES, Richard. "The London Sugar Market, 1740-1769." *Econ Hist Rev,* IX (1956), 254-270.

7 PARES, Richard. *Merchants and Planters.* See **53**.10.

8 PARES, Richard. *War and Trade in the West Indies, 1739-1763.* Oxford, 1936.

9 PARES, Richard. *A West-India Fortune.* New York, 1950.

10 PARES, Richard. *Yankees and Creoles. The Trade Between North America and the West Indies before the American Revolution.* London, 1956.

11 SHERIDAN, Richard B. "The Molasses Act and the Market Strategy of the British Sugar Planters." *J Econ Hist,* XVII (1957), 62-83.

12 VAN DUSEN, Albert E. "Colonial Connecticut's Trade with the West Indies." *N Eng Soc Stu Bull,* XIII (1956), 11-30.

The Indian Trade

13 BROSHAR, Helen. "The First Push Westward of the Albany Traders." *Miss Val Hist Rev,* VII (1920), 228-241.

14 BUFFINTON, Arthur H. "The Policy of Albany and English Westward Expansion." *Miss Val Hist Rev,* VIII (1922), 327-366.

15 CRANE, Verner W. *The Southern Frontier.* See **18**.17.

16 FANT, H. B. "The Indian Trade Policy of the Trustees for Establishing the Colony of Georgia in America." *Ga Hist Q,* XV (1931), 207-222.

17 FRANKLIN, W. Neil. "Pennsylvania-Virginia Rivalry for the Indian Trade of the Ohio Valley." *Miss Val Hist Rev,* XX (1934), 463-480.

18 FRANKLIN, W. Neil. "Virginia and the Cherokee Indian Trade, 1673-1752." *E Tenn Hist Soc Pub,* IV (1932), 3-21.

19 FRANKLIN, W. Neil. "Virginia and the Cherokee Indian Trade, 1753-1775." *E Tenn Hist Soc Pub,* V (1933), 22-38.

20 JACOBS, Wilbur R. "Unsavory Sidelights on the Colonial Fur Trade." *N Y Hist,* XXXIV (1953), 135-148.

21 JENNINGS, Francis. "The Indian Trade of the Susquehanna Valley." *Proc Am Philos Soc,* CX (1966), 406-424.

22 LEACH, Douglas E. *The Northern Frontier.* See **19**.8.

23 MACFARLANE, Ronald O. "The Massachusetts Bay Truck-Houses in Diplomacy with the Indians." *N Eng Q,* XI (1938), 48-65.

1 NASH, Gary B. "The Quest for the Susquehanna Valley: New York, Pennsylvania, and the Seventeenth-Century Fur Trade." *N Y Hist,* XLVIII (1967), 3-27.

2 PHILLIPS, Paul. *The Fur Trade.* Norman, Okla., 1961.

3 PIETRASZEK, Bernadine. "Anglo-French Trade Conflicts in North America, 1702-1713." *Mid-Am,* XXXV (1953), 144-174.

4 WILLIAMS, Meade C. "The Early Fur Trade in North America." *Mich Hist Soc Coll,* XXXV (1907), 58-73.

5 WITTHOFT, John. "Archaeology as a Key to the Colonial Fur Trade." *Minn Hist,* XL (1966), 203-209.

Illegal Trade

6 JOHNSON, Victor L. "Fair Traders and Smugglers in Philadelphia, 1754-1763." *Pa Mag Hist,* LXXXIII (1959), 125-149.

7 LUNN, Jean. "The Illegal Fur Trade out of New France, 1713-1760." *Canad Hist Assn Rep,* 1939 (1939), 61-76.

8 MORGAN, Edmund S. "An Anonymous Poem." *Book at Brown,* XV (1953), 1-6.

9 PYRKE, Berne A. "The Secret Compact of the Albany and Montreal Fur Traders, 1701." *Galleon,* XI (1953), 3-7.

10 TOWLE, Dorothy S. "Smuggling Canary Wine in 1740." *N Eng Q,* VI (1933), 144-154.

Privateering and Piracy

11 CHAPIN, Howard M. *Privateer Ships and Sailors The First Century of American Colonial Privateering, 1625-1725.* Toulon, 1926.

12 CHAPIN, Howard M. *Privateering in King George's War, 1739-1748.* Providence, R. I., 1928.

13 DOW, George F. and John H. EDMONDS. *The Pirates of the New England Coast, 1630-1730.* Salem, Mass., 1923.

14 HUGHSON, Shirley C. "The Carolina Pirates and Colonial Commerce, 1670-1740." *Hop U Stud,* XII (1894), 1-134.

15 JAMESON, John F., ed. *Privateering and Piracy in the Colonial Period: Illustrative Documents.* New York, 1923.

16 WILLIAMS, Lloyd H. *Pirates of Colonial Virginia.* Richmond, Va., 1937.

Intercolonial Trade

17 CRAWFORD, Walter F. "The Commerce of Rhode Island with the Southern Continental Colonies in the Eighteenth Century." *R I Hist Soc Coll,* XIV (1921), 99-110, 124-130.

18 NETTELS, Curtis. "The Economic Relations of Boston, Philadelphia, and New York, 1680-1715." *J Econ Bus Hist,* III (1931), 185-215.

19 SACHS, William S. "Interurban Correspondents and the Development of a National Economy before the Revolution: New York as a Case Study." *N Y Hist,* XXXVI (1955), 320-335.

20 WRIGHT, Richardson. *Hawkers and Walkers in Early America. . . .* Philadelphia, 1927.

Internal Trade and Small Business

1 BAXTER, William T. "Daniel Henchman, a Colonial Bookseller." *Essex Inst Hist Coll,* LXX (1934), 1-30.

2 LEMON, James T. "Urbanization and the Development of Eighteenth-Century Southeastern Pennsylvania and Adjacent Delaware." See **49**.2.

3 MERRENS, H. Roy. *Colonial North Carolina. See* **25**.19.

4 PLUMMER, Wilbur C. "Consumer Credit in Colonial Pennsylvania." *Pa Mag Hist,* LXVI (1942), 385-409.

5 RAWSON, Marion N. *Handwrought Ancestors: The Story of Early American Shops and Those Who Worked Therein.* New York, 1936.

The Role of the Merchants

General

6 BRUCHEY, Stuart, ed. *The Colonial Merchant. Sources and Readings.* New York, 1966.†

7 HALL, Charles W. "The Merchant from the Time of the Discovery of America up to the Time of the American Revolution." *Nat Mag,* XXXIV (1911), 802-818.

8 HARRINGTON, Virginia D. "The Place of the Merchant in New York Colonial Life." *N Y Hist,* XIII (1932), 366-380.

Emergent Groups

9 BAILYN, Bernard. "Kinship and Trade in Seventeenth Century New England." *Explor Entrep Hist,* VI (1954), 197-205.

10 BAILYN, Bernard. *The New England Merchants in the Seventeenth Century.* Cambridge, Mass., 1955.†

11 FREUND, Miriam K. *Jewish Merchants in Colonial America, their Achievements and their Contributions to the Development of America.* New York, 1939.

12 HARRINGTON, Virginia D. *The New York Merchant on the Eve of the Revolution.* New York, 1935.

13 KOHLER, M. J. "Jewish Activity in American Colonial Commerce." *Am Jew Hist Soc Pub,* X (1902), 47-64.

14 SELLERS, Leila. *Charleston Business on the Eve of the Revolution.* Chapel Hill, 1934.

15 TOLLES, Frederick B. "Benjamin Franklin's Business Mentors: The Philadelphia Quakers." *Wm Mar Q,* 3rd ser., IV (1947), 60-69.

16 TOLLES, Frederick B. *Meeting House and Counting House, 1682-1763.* See **34**.1.

Studies of Individual Merchants and Firms

17 BAXTER, William T. *The House of Hancock, Business in Boston, 1724-1775.* Cambridge, Mass., 1945.

18 BIGELOW, Bruce M. "Aaron Lopez, Colonial Merchant of Newport." *N Eng Q,* IV (1931), 757-776.

19 CLARK, William B. "The John Ashmead Story, 1738-1818." *Pa Mag Hist,* LXXXI (1958), 3-54.

20 DONNAN, Elizabeth. "Eighteenth-Century English Merchants. Micajah Perry." *J Econ Bus Hist,* IV (1931), 70-98.

1 EDELMAN, Edward. "Thomas Hancock, Colonial Merchant." *J Econ Bus Hist,* I (1928), 77-104.

2 FAIRCHILD, Byron. *Messrs. William Pepperrell. Merchants at Piscataqua.* Ithaca, 1954.

3 HEDGES, James B. *The Browns of Providence Plantations.* Vol. I, *Colonial Years.* Cambridge, Mass., 1952.

4 HUHNER, Leon. "Daniel Gomez, a Pioneer Merchant of Early New York." *Am Jew Hist Soc Pub,* XLI (1951), 107-125.

5 JAHER, Frederic C. "Businessman and Gentlemen: Nathan and Thomas Gold Appleton—An Exploration in Intergenerational History." *Explor Entrep Hist,* IV (1966), 17-39.

6 LEDER, Lawrence H. and Vincent P. CAROSSO. "Robert Livingston. Business man of Colonial New York." *Bus Hist Rev,* XXX (1956), 18-45.

7 MORISON, Samuel E. "The Letter-Book of Hugh Hall, Merchant of Barbados, 1716-1720." *Pub Col Soc Mass,* XXXII (1937), 514-521.

8 PHILLIPS, James D. *The Life and Times of Richard Derby, Merchant of Salem, 1712 to 1783.* Cambridge, Mass., 1929.

9 ROBERTS, William I., III. "Ralph Carr: A Newcastle Merchant and the American Colonial Trade." *Bus Hist Rev,* XLII (1968), 271-287.

10 ROBERTS, William L., III. "Samuel Storke: An Eighteenth-Century London Merchant Trading to the American Colonies." *Bus Hist Rev,* XXXIX (1965), 147-170.

11 TAPLEY, Harriet S. "Richard Skinner, an Early Eighteenth-Century Merchant of Marblehead, with Some Account of his Family." *Essex Inst Hist Coll,* LXVII (1931), 329-352.

12 WALL, A. J. "Samuel Loudon (1727-1813) (Merchant, Printer, and Patriot) with some of his Letters." *N-Y Hist Soc Q,* VI (1922), 75-92.

13 WEAVER, Glenn. *Jonathan Trumbull, Connecticut's Merchant Magistrate, 1710-1785.* Hartford, Conn., 1956.

14 WENDELL, William G. *Jonathan Warner: Merchant and Trader, King's Councillor, Mariner, Jurist.* New York, 1950.

15 WHITE, Philip L. *The Beekmans of New York in Politics and Commerce, 1647-1877 . . . with an Introduction by Fenwick Beekman.* New York, 1956.

16 WHITE, Philip L., ed *The Beekman Mercantile Papers, 1746-1799.* 3 vols. New York, 1956.

Prices and Consumption

17 BEZANSON, Anne, Robert D. GRAY, and Miriam HUSSEY. *Prices in Colonial Pennsylvania.* Philadelphia, 1935.

18 COLE, Arthur H. *Statistical Supplement: Actual Wholesale Prices of Various Commodities.* Cambridge, Mass., 1938.

19 COLE, Arthur H. *Wholesale Commodity Prices in the United States, 1700-1861.* Cambridge, Mass., 1938.

20 LEMON, James T. "Household Consumption in Eighteenth Century America and its Relationship to Production and Trade: The Situation among Farmers in Southeastern Pennsylvania." *Ag Hist,* XLI (1967), 67-70.

1 TAYLOR, George R. "Wholesale Commodity Prices at Charleston, South Carolina, 1732-1791; 1796-1861." *J Econ Bus Hist,* IV (1932), 356-377, 848-868.

THE STRUCTURE OF OPPORTUNITY: MANUFACTURING

General

2 BISHOP, James L. *History of American Manufactures, 1608-1860.* 3rd ed. 3 vols. Philadelphia, 1867.

3 CLARK, Victor S. *History of Manufactures in the United States.* 3 vols. New York, 1929.

4 NICHOLS, Jeanette P. "Colonial Industries of New Jersey, 1618-1815." *Am,* XXIV (1930), 299-342.

5 TRYON, Rolla M. *Household Manufacture in the United States, 1640-1860.* Chicago, 1917.

Specialized Studies

Agricultural Industries

6 GALLOWAY, J. H. "The Sugar Industry in Barbados during the 17th Century." *J Trop Geog,* XIX (1964), 35-41.

7 PRICE, Jacob M. "The Beginnings of Tobacco Manufacture in Virginia." *Va Mag Hist,* LXIV (1956), 3-29.

8 WEAVER, Glenn. "Industry in an Agrarian Economy: Early Eighteenth Century Connecticut." *Bull Conn Hist Soc,* XIX (1954), 82-92.

9 WEISS, Harry B. and Robert J. SIM. *The Early Grist and Flouring Mills of New Jersey.* Trenton, N.J., 1956.

Silk Culture

10 HAMER, Marguerite. "The Foundation and Failure of the Silk Industry in Provincial Georgia." *N C Hist Rev,* XII (1935), 125-148.

11 MC KINSTRY, Mary T. "Silk Culture in the Colony of Georgia." *Ga Hist Q,* XIV (1930), 225-235.

12 STEPHENS, Pauline T. "Silk Industry in Georgia." *Ga Rev,* VII (1953), 39-49.

Textiles

13 WEISS, Harry B. and Grace M. ZIEGLER. *The Early Fulling Mills of New Jersey.* Trenton, N.J., 1957.

Forest Industries: Naval Stores, Shipbuilding, Lumber, and Paper
For additional references see the section on Naval Stores and Forest Policy under The British Background: Relations with the Colonies.

14 CHANDLER, Charles Lyon. *Early Shipbuilding in Pennsylvania, 1683-1812.* Philadelphia, 1932.

15 EVANS, Cerinda Weatherly, *Some Notes on Shipbuilding and Shipping in Colonial Virginia.* (Jamestown 350th Anniversary Historical Booklet 22). Williamsburg, Va., 1957.

16 GILLINGHAM, Harrold E. "Some Colonial Ships Built in Philadelphia." *Pa Mag Hist,* LVI (1932), 156-186.

17 HUNTER, Dard. *Paper Making in Pioneer America.* Philadelphia, 1952.

1 MERRENS, H. Roy. *Colonial North Carolina.* See **25**.19.

2 SMYTH, Lawrence T. "The Lumber Industry in Maine." *N Eng Mag,* XXV (1901-1902), 629-648.

3 SNOW, Sinclair. "Naval Stores in Colonial Virginia." *Va Mag Hist,* LXXII (1964), 75-93.

Fishing and Whaling

4 DODGE, Stanley D. "The Geography of the Codfishing Industry in Colonial New England." *Phila Geog Soc Bull,* XXV (1927), 43-50.

5 HORMAN, Elmo P. *The American Whaleman: A Study of Life and Labor in the Whaling Industry.* New York, 1928.

6 PALMER, William R. "Early American Whaling." *Historian,* XXII (1959), 1-8.

7 PEARSON, John C. "The Fish and Fisheries of Colonial Virginia." *Wm Mar Q,* 2nd ser., XXII (1942), 213-220, 353-360; XXIII (1943), 1-7, 130-135; 3rd ser., I (1944), 179-183.

8 STACKPOLE, Edouard A. *William Rotch (1734-1828) Nantucket: America's Pioneer in International Industry.* New York, 1950.

9 TOWER, Walter S. *A History of the American Whale Fishery.* Philadelphia, 1907.

Iron, Lead, and Gunpowder

10 BERKEBILE, Don H. "The Gun Powder Industry in Colonial America." *Muzzle Blasts,* X (1948), 18-19, 23, 26-27.

11 BINING, Arthur Cecil. "Early Ironmasters of Pennsylvania." *Pa Hist,* XVIII (1951), 93-103.

12 BINING, Arthur Cecil. "The Iron Plantations of Early Pennsylvania." *Pa Mag Hist,* LVII (1933), 117-137.

13 BOYER, Charles S. *Early Forges and Furnaces in New Jersey.* Philadelphia, 1931.

14 HECHT, Arthur. "Lead Production in Virginia during the Seventeenth and Eighteenth Centuries." *W Va Hist,* XXV (1964), 173-183.

15 JOHNSON, Keach. "The Baltimore Company Seeks English Markets: A Study of the Anglo-American Iron Trade, 1731-1755." *Wm Mar Q,* 3rd ser., XVI (1959), 37-60.

16 JOHNSON, Keach. "The Baltimore Company Seeks English Subsidies for the Colonial Iron Industry." *Md Hist Mag,* XLVI (1951), 27-43.

17 JOHNSON, Keach. "The Gensis of the Baltimore Ironworks." *J S Hist,* XIX (1953), 157-179.

18 NELSON, William. "Beginnings of the Iron Industry in Trenton, New Jersey—1723-1750." *Pa Mag Hist,* XXXV (1911), 228-243.

19 NEU, Irene D. "The Iron Plantations of Colonial New York." *N Y Hist,* XXXIII (1952), 3-24.

Craft Industries

General

20 BRIDENBAUGH, Carl. *The Colonial Craftsman.* New York, 1950.†

21 MC ANEAR, Beverly. "The Place of the Freeman in Old New York." *N Y Hist,* XXI (1940), 418-430.

1 STAVISKY, Leonard P. "Negro Craftsmanship in Early America." *Am Hist Rev,* LIV (1949), 315-325.

2 WALSH, Richard. *Charleston's Sons of Liberty: A Study of the Artisans, 1763-1789.* Columbia, S.C., 1959.

Metalworking
For additional references see the section on Metalworking under Culture: The Fine Arts.

3 BUHLER, Kathryn C. *Paul Revere, Goldsmith, 1735-1818.* Boston, 1956.

4 CLARKE, Hermann F. *John Coney, Silversmith, 1655-1722.* Boston, 1932.

5 FRENCH, Hollis. *Jacob Hurd and His Sons, Nathaniel & Benjamin, Silversmiths, 1702-1781.* Walpole Society, 1939.

6 GILLINGHAM, Harrold E. "Caesar Ghiselin, Philadelphia's First Gold and Silversmith, 1693-1733." *Pa Mag Hist,* LVII (1933), 244-259.

7 HASTINGS, Mrs. Russell. "Peter Van Dyck of New York, Goldsmith, 1684-1750." *Antiques,* XXXI (1937), 236-239, 302-305.

8 KAUFFMAN, Henry J. "Coppersmithing in Pennsylvania: Being a Treatise on the Art of the Eighteenth Century Coppersmith. . . ." *Pa Ger Folk Soc Yr Bk,* XI (1946), 83-153.

9 ROSENBAUM, Jeanette W. *Myer Myers, Goldsmith, 1723-1795.* Philadelphia, 1954.

10 SMITH, Helen B. "Nicholas Roosevelt—Goldsmith (1715-1769." *N-Y Hist Soc Q,* XXXIV (1950), 301-314.

11 WROTH, Lawrence C. *Abel Buell of Connecticut: Silversmith, Type Founder and Engraver.* Middletown, Conn., 1958.

Glassmaking and Ceramics

12 GILLINGHAM, Harrold E. "Pottery, China, and Glassmaking in Philadelphia." *Pa Mag Hist,* LIV (1930), 97-129.

13 WELLS, E. D. "Duche, the Potter." *Ga Hist Q,* XLI (1957), 383-390.

Other

14 ECKHARDT, George Henry. *Pennsylvania Clocks and Clockmakers: Epic of Early American Science, Industry, and Craftsmanship.* New York, 1955.

15 SWAN, Mabel M. "Elijah and Jacob Sanderson, Early Salem Cabinetmakers; a Salem Eighteenth Century Furniture Trust Company." *Essex Inst Hist Coll,* LXX (1934), 323-364.

16 WITTLINGER, Carlton O. "The Small Arms Industry of Lancaster County, 1710-1840." *Pa Hist,* XXIV (1957), 121-136.

THE STRUCTURE OF OPPORTUNITY: THE PROFESSIONS

General

17 BOORSTIN, Daniel J. *The Americans: The Colonial Experience.* See **22.5.**

The Clergy

18 BAINTON, Roland. *Yale and the Ministry.* New Haven, 1955.

19 GAMBRELL, Mary Latimer. *Ministerial Training in Eighteenth-Century New England.* New York, 1937.

1 MEAD, Sidney. "The Rise of the Evangelical Conception of the Ministry in America: 1607-1850," in *The Ministry in Historical Perspective,* ed. Richard Niebuhr and others. New York, 1956.

2 SHEWMAKER, William O. "The Training of the Protestant Ministry in the United States of America, before the Establishment of the Theological Seminaries." *Pa P Am Soc Ch Hist,* 2nd ser., VI (1921), 71-197.

3 SHIPTON, Clifford K. "The New England Clergy of the 'Glacial Age.'" *Pub Col Soc Mass,* XXXII (1937), 24-54.

The Law

4 CHESTER, Alden. *Courts and Lawyers of New York: A History, 1609-1925.* 3 vols. New York, 1925.

5 CHROUST, Anton-Hermann. *The Rise of the Legal Profession in America.* Vol. I, *The Colonial Experience.* Norman, Okla., 1965.

6 EASTMAN, Frank M. *Courts and Lawyers of Pennsylvania; a History, 1623-1923.* New York, 1922.

7 GORDON, Armistead C. "Some Lawyers in Colonial Virginia." In the *Proceedings of the Thirty-Second Annual Meeting of the Virginia State Bar Association . . . 1921,* 140-159. Richmond, Va., 1921.

8 HAMILTON, J. G. De Roulhac. "Southern Members of the Inns of Court." *N C Hist Rev,* X (1933), 273-286.

9 HAMLIN, Paul M. *Legal Education in Colonial New York.* New York, 1939.

10 HASKINS, George L. "Law and Colonial Society." *Am Q,* IX (1957), 354-364.

11 HOLT, W. Stull. "Charles Carroll, Barrister: The Man." *Md Hist Mag,* XXXI (1936), 112-126.

12 HURST, James Willard. *The Growth of American Law: The Law Makers.* Boston, 1950.

13 JONES, E. Alfred. *American Members of the Inns of Court.* London, 1924.

14 KEASBEY, Edward Q. *The Courts and Lawyers of New Jersey 1661-1912.* 3 vols. New York, 1912.

15 KLEIN, Milton M. "The Rise of the New York Bar: The Legal Career of William Livingston." *Wm Mar Q,* 3rd ser., XV (1958), 334-358.

16 MAC CRACKEN, Henry N. *Prologue to Independence: The Trials of James Alexander, American, 1715-1756.* New York, 1964.

17 NIX, Foster C. "Andrew Hamilton's Early Years in the American Colonies." *Wm Mar Q,* 3rd ser., XXI (1964), 390-407.

18 REED, George B. *Sketch of the Life of the Honorable John Read, of Boston, 1722-1749.* Boston, 1903.

19 WARREN, Charles. *A History of the American Bar.* Boston, 1911.

Medicine
For additional references see the section on Medicine under Culture: Science.

20 BARTLETT, Charles J. "Medical Licensure in Connecticut." *Conn Med J,* VI (1942), 182-190.

1 BEALL, Otho and Richard H. SHRYOCK. *Cotton Mather, First Significant Figure in American Medicine.* Baltimore, 1954.

2 BEINFIELD, Malcolm S. "The Early New England Doctor: An Adaptation to a Provincial Environment." *Yale J Biol Med,* XV (1942), 271-288.

3 BELL, Whitfield J., Jr. *John Morgan: Continental Doctor.* Philadelphia, 1965.

4 BELL, Whitfield J., Jr. "Medical Practice in Colonial America." *Bull Hist Med,* XXXI (1957), 442-453.

5 CORNER, Betsy Copping. *William Shippen, Jr., Pioneer in American Medical Education: A Biographical Essay.* Philadelphia, 1951.

6 DUFFY, John. *Epidemics in Colonial America.* Baton Rouge, La., 1953.

7 EZELL, Stiles D. "Regulation and Licensing of Physicians in New York." *N Y J Med,* LVII (1957), 543-554.

8 GROCE, George C., Jr. "Benjamin Gale." *N Eng Q,* X (1937), 697-716.

9 LONG, Dorothy. "Early North Carolina Medicine: Physicians of the Colonial Period." *N C Med J,* XIII (1952), 347-348, 577-578.

10 LONG, Dorothy. "Early North Carolina Medicine: Some Eighteenth Century Physicians." *N C Med J,* XIV (1953), 432-433.

11 LONG, Dorothy. "Medical Education in Early North Carolina." *N C Med J,* XV (1954), 519-520.

12 MILLER, Genevieve. "Medical Apprenticeship in the American Colonies." *Ciba,* VIII (1947), 502-510.

13 MILLER, Genevieve. "Medical Education in the American Colonies." *J Med Ed,* XXXI (1956), 82-94.

14 MILLER, Genevieve. "Medical Schools in the Colonies." *Ciba,* VIII (1947), 522-532.

15 POSTELL, William D. "Medical Education and Medical Schools in Colonial America." *Int Rec Med,* CLXXI (1958), 364-370.

16 THOMS, Herbert. "The Doctor in Colonial Connecticut." *Conn Med J,* XX (1956), 986-988.

17 THOMS, Herbert. *The Doctors Jared of Connecticut: Jared Eliot, Jared Potter, Jared Kirtland.* Hamden, Conn., 1958.

Printing

18 DE ARMOND, Anna J. *Andrew Bradford: Colonial Journalist.* Newark, Del., 1949.

19 DURNBAUGH, Donald F. "Christopher Sauer, Pennsylvania-German Printer: His Youth in Germany and Later Relationships with Europe." *Pa Mag Hist,* LXXXII (1958), 316-340.

20 FORD, Paul L., ed. *Journals of Hugh Gaine, Printer.* 2 vols. New York, 1902.

21 MC CULLOCH, William. "William McCulloch's Additions to Thomas's History of Printing." *Proc Am Ant Soc,* n ser., XXXI (1921), 89-247.

22 MC MURTRIE, Douglas C. *A History of Printing in the United States; The Story of the Introduction of the Press and of its History and Influence during the Pioneer Period in Each State of the Union.* New York, 1936.

1 MC MURTRIE, Douglas C. *The Pioneer Printer of Georgia.* Chicago, 1930.

2 PARKER, Peter J. "The Philadelphia Printer: A Study of an Eighteenth-Century Businessman." *Bus Hist Rev,* XL (1966), 24-46.

3 SILVER, Rollo G. "Government Printing in Massachusetts Bay, 1700-1750." *Proc Am Ant Soc,* LXVIII (1958), 135-162.

4 SILVER, Rollo G. "Publishing in Boston, 1726-1757: The Accounts of Daniel Henchman." *Proc Am Ant Soc,* LXVI (1956), 17-36.

5 THOMAS, Isaiah. *History of Printing in America, with a Biography of Printers.* 2nd ed., with author's corrections and additions. 2 vols. Albany, N.Y., 1874.

6 WALL, Alexander J., Jr. "William Bradford, Colonial Printer—A Tercentenary Review." *Proc Am Ant Soc,* LXXIII (1963), 361-384.

7 WOLF, Edwin, II. "B. Franklin, Printer." *Ala Bull,* L (1956), 13-16.

8 WROTH, Lawrence C. *The Colonial Printer.* New York, 1931.†

9 WROTH, Lawrence C. *William Parks, Printer and Journalist of England and Colonial America; with a List of the Issues of his Several Presses and a Facsimile of the Earliest Virginia Imprint Known to be in Existence.* Richmond, Va., 1926.

Teaching

10 BRUMBAUGH, Martin G. *The Life and Works of Christopher Dock.* Philadelphia, 1908.

11 ELSBREE, Willard S. *The American Teacher.* New York, 1939.

THE PROBLEMS OF ECONOMIC LIFE

Labor

General

12 Bureau of Labor Statistics. *Wages in the Colonial Period.* (Bulletin 499.) Washington, D.C., 1929.

13 DULLES, Foster R. *Labor in America: A History.* New York, 1949.

14 JERNEGAN, Marcus W. *Laboring and Dependent Classes in Colonial America. . . .* Chicago, 1931.

15 JONAS, Manfred. "Wages in Early Colonial Maryland." *Md Hist Mag,* LI (1956), 27-38.

16 MC KEE, Samuel, Jr. *Labor in Colonial New York, 1664-1776.* New York, 1935.

17 MORRIS, Richard B. *Government and Labor in Early America.* New York, 1946.†

18 MORRIS, Richard B. and Jonathan GROSSMAN. "The Regulation of Wages in Early Massachusetts." *N Eng Q,* XI (1938), 470-500.

White Servitude

1 BALLAGH, James C. *White Servitude in the Colony of Virginia: A Study of Indentured Labor in the American Colonies.* Baltimore, 1895.

2 GEISER, K. F. *Redemptions and Indentured Servants in the Colony and Commonwealth of Pennsylvania.* New Haven, 1901.

3 HAAR, Charles M. "White Indentured Servants in Colonial New York." *Am,* XXXIV (1940), 370-392.

4 HENNIGHAUSEN, L. P. "The Redemptioners and the German Society of Maryland." *Soc Hist Ger Md,* 2nd Annual Report (1887-1888), 33-54.

5 HERRICK, Cheesman A. *White Servitude in Pennsylvania: Indentured and Redemption Labor in Colony and Commonwealth.* Philadelphia, 1926.

6 MC CORMAC, Eugene I. *White Servitude in Maryland, 1634-1820.* Baltimore, 1904.

7 SEARS, William P., Jr. "Indentured Servants in Colonial America." *Dal Rev,* XXXVII (1957), 121-140.

8 SMITH, Abbot Emerson. *Colonists in Bondage: White Servitude and Convict Labor in America 1607-1776.* Chapel Hill, 1947.

9 SMITH, Warren B. *White Servitude in Colonial South Carolina.* Columbia, S.C., 1961.

10 SOLLERS, Basil. "Transported Convict Laborers in Maryland During the Colonial Period." *Md Hist Mag,* II (1907), 17-47.

11 STUART, William. "White Servitude in New York and New Jersey." *Am,* XV (1921), 19-37.

12 TOWNER, Lawrence W. "A Fondness for Freedom: Servant Protest in Puritan Society." *Wm Mar Q,* 3rd ser., XIX (1962), 201-219.

Indian Slavery

13 LAUBER, Almon W. *Indian Slavery in Colonial Times Within the Present Limits of the United States.* New York, 1913.

14 WINSTON, Sanford. "Indian Slavery in the Carolina Region." *J Neg Hist,* XIX (1934), 431-440.

African Slavery

15 BALLAGH, James C. *A History of Slavery in Virginia.* Baltimore, 1902.

16 BENNETT, J. Harry. *Bishops and Bondsmen: Slavery and Apprenticeship on Codrington Plantations of Barbados, 1710-1838.* Berkeley, Calif., 1958.

17 BENNETT, J. Harry, Jr. "The Problem of Slave Labor Supply at the Codrington Plantations." *J Neg Hist,* XXXVI (1951), 406-441; XXXVII (1952), 115-141.

18 CLARK, Ernest J., Jr. "Aspects of the North Carolina Slave Code, 1715-1860." *N C Hist Rev,* XXXIX (1962), 148-164.

19 DEGLER, Carl N. "Slavery and the Genesis of American Race Prejudice." *Comp Stud Soc Hist,* II (1959), 49-66.

20 ELKINS, Stanley M. and Eric MC KITRICK. "Institutions and the Law of Slavery: The Dynamics of Unopposed Capitalism." *Am Q,* IX (1957), 3-21.

1 ELKINS, Stanley M. and Eric MC KITRICK. "Institutions and the Law of Slavery: Slavery in Capitalist and Non-Capitalist Cultures." *Am Q,* IX (1957), 159-179.

2 FRANKLIN, John Hope. *From Slavery to Freedom: A History of American Negroes.* 2nd ed. New York, 1956.

3 GOVEIA, Elsa V. *Slave Society in the British Leeward Islands at the End of the Eighteenth Century.* New Haven, Conn., 1965.

4 GRANT, Douglas. *The Fortunate Slave: An Illustration of African Slavery in the Early Eighteenth Century.* London, 1968.

5 HANDLIN, Oscar and Mary. "The Origins of the Southern Labor System." *Wm Mar Q,* 3rd ser., VII (1950), 199-222.

6 HAYWOOD, C. Robert. "Mercantilism and Colonial Slave Labor, 1700-1763." *J S Hist,* XXIII (1957), 454-464.

7 HIGHAM, C. S. S. "The Negro Policy of Christopher Coddrington." *J Neg Hist,* X (1925), 150-153.

8 HOETINK, H. *The Two Variants in Caribbean Race Relations: A Contribution to the Sociology of Segmented Societies.* London, 1967.

9 JERNEGAN, Marcus W. "Slavery and the Beginnings of Industrialism in the American Colonies." *Am Hist Rev,* XXV (1920), 220-240.

10 JORDAN, Winthrop D. "Modern Tensions and the Origins of American Slavery." *J S Hist,* XXVII (1952), 18-33.

11 KLEIN, Herbert S. "Anglicization, Catholocism and the Negro Slave." *Comp Stud Soc Hist,* VIII (1966), 295-327. Comment by Elsa V. Goevia, *Ibid,* 328-330.

12 KLEIN, Herbert S. *Slavery in the Americas: A Comparative Study of Cuba and Virginia.* Chicago, 1967.

13 MC CRADY, Edward. "Slavery in the Province of South Carolina (1670-1770)." *Am Hist Assn Ann Rep,* (1895), 631-673.

14 MC MANUS, Edgar J. *A History of Negro Slavery in New York.* Syracuse, N.Y., 1966.

15 MITCHELL, Mary H. "Slavery in Connecticut and Especially in New Haven." *Pap N Haven Col Hist Soc,* X (1951), 286-312.

16 MOSS, Simeon F. "The Persistence of Slavery and Involuntary Servitude in a Free State (1685-1866)." *J Neg Hist,* XXXV (1950), 289-314.

17 MUNROE, John A. "The Negro in Delaware." *S Atl Q,* LVI (1957), 428-444.

18 PADGETT, James A. "The Status of Slaves in Colonial North Carolina." *J Neg Hist,* XIV (1929), 300-327.

19 PALMER, Paul C. "Servant into Slave: The Evolution of the Legal Status of the Negro Laborer in Colonial Virginia." *S Atl Q,* LXV (1966), 355-370.

20 PHILLIPS, U. B. *American Negro Slavery. . . .* New York, 1918.†

21 PITMAN, Frank W. "Slavery on the British West India Plantations in the Eighteenth Century." *J Neg Hist,* XI (1926), 584-668.

22 POSTELL, William D. *The Health of Slaves on Southern Plantations.* Baton Rouge, La., 1951.

23 SIO, Arnold A. "Interpretations of Slavery: The Slave Status in the Americas." *Comp Stud Soc Hist,* VII (1965), 289-308.

24 SIRMANS, M. Eugene, "The Legal Status of the Slave in South Carolina, 1670-1740." *J S Hist,* XXVIII (1926), 462-473.

1 STUART, William. "Negro Slavery in New Jersey and New York." *Am,* XVI (1922), 347-367.

2 TURNER, Edward Raymond. "Slavery in Colonial Pennsylvania." *Pa Mag Hist,* XXV (1911), 141-151.

3 WAX, Darold D. "Georgia and the Negro Before the American Revolution." *Ga Hist Q,* LI (1967), 63-77.

Slave Revolts

4 APTHEKER, Herbert. *American Negro Slave Revolts.* New York, 1943.†

5 CLARKE, T. Wood. "The Negro Plot of 1741." *N Y Hist,* XXV (1944), 167-181.

6 SCOTT, Kenneth. "The Slave Insurrection in New York in 1712." *N-Y Hist Soc Q,* XLV (1961), 43-74.

7 SZASZ, Ferenc M. "The New York Slave Revolt of 1741: A Re-Examination." *N Y Hist,* XLVIII (1967), 215-230.

Anti-Slavery Impulse

8 CARROLL, Kenneth L. "Maryland Quakers and Slavery." *Md Hist Mag,* XLV (1950), 215-225.

9 CARROLL, Kenneth L. "Religious Influences on the Manumission of Slaves in Caroline, Dorchester, and Talbot Counties." *Md Hist Mag,* LVI (1961), 176-197.

10 CARROLL, Kenneth L. "William Southeby, Early Quaker Antislavery Writer." *Pa Mag Hist,* LXXXIX (1965), 416-427.

11 DAVIS, David B. *The Problem of Slavery in Western Culture.* Ithaca, 1966.

12 DRAKE, Thomas E. *Quakers and Slavery in America.* New Haven, 1950.

13 FANT, H. B. "The Labor Policy of the Trustees for Establishing the Colony of Georgia in America." *Ga Hist Q,* XVI (1932), 1-16.

14 LOCKE, Mary S. *Anti-Slavery in America from the Introduction of African Slaves to the Prohibition of the Slave Trade (1619-1808).* Boston, 1901.

15 MOULTON, Phillips. "John Woolman's Approach to Social Action, As Exemplified in Relation to Slavery." *Ch Hist,* XXXV (1966), 399-410.

16 PANNIER, Jacques. *Antoine Bénézez (de Saint-Quentin), un Quaker français en Amérique.* Toulouse, 1925.

17 TOWNER, Lawrence W. "The Sewall-Saffin Dialogue on Slavery." *Wm Mar Q,* 3rd ser., XXI (1964), 40-52.

18 WOOLMAN, John. *Journal and Essays . . . 1720-1772.* Ed. Amelia Mott Gummere. Philadelphia, 1922.

19 WYNDHAM, Hugh A. *The Atlantic and Slavery. . . . A Report in the Study Group Series of the Royal Institute of International Affairs.* London, 1935.

Money

General

20 ADLER, Simon L. "Money and Money Units in the American Colonies." *Pub Roch Hist Soc,* VIII (1929), 143-173.

1 BULLOCK, Charles J. *Essays on the Monetary History of the United States.* New York, 1900.

2 NETTELS, Curtis P. "British Payments in the American Colonies, 1685-1715." *Eng Hist Rev,* CLXXXIX (1933), 229-249.

3 NETTELS, Curtis P. *The Money Supply of the American Colonies before 1720.* Madison, Wis., 1934.

Paper Currency Experiments

4 BEHRENS, Kathryn L. *Paper Money in Maryland, 1727-1789.* Baltimore, 1923.

5 BURSTEIN, M. L. "Colonial Currency and Contemporary Monetary Theory: A Review Article." *Explor Entrep Hist,* 2nd ser., III (1966), 220-233.

6 DAVIS, Andrew M. *Currency and Banking in the Province of Massachusetts-Bay.* 2 vols. New York, 1901.

7 FERGUSON, E. James. "Currency Finance: An Interpretation of Colonial Monetary Practices." *Wm Mar Q,* 3rd ser., X (1953), 153-180.

8 FREIBERG, Malcolm. "Thomas Hutchinson and the Province Currency." *N Eng Q,* XXX (1957), 190-208.

9 GOULD, Clarence P. *Money and Transportation in Maryland, 1720-1765.* Baltimore, 1915.

10 HEATH, William E. "The Early Colonial Money System of Georgia." *Ga Hist Q,* XIX (1935), 145-160.

11 JELLISON, Richard M. "Antecedents of the South Carolina Currency Acts of 1736 and 1746." *Wm Mar Q,* 3rd ser., XVI (1959), 556-567.

12 JELLISON, Richard M. "Paper Currency in Colonial South Carolina: A Reappraisal." *S C Hist Mag,* LXII (1961), 134-147.

13 KEMMERER, Donald L. "The Colonial Loan-Office System in New Jersey." *J Pol Econ,* XLVII (1939), 867-874.

14 KEMMERER, Donald L. "A History of Paper Money in Colonial New Jersey, 1668-1775." *Proc N J Hist Soc,* LXXIV (1956), 107-144.

15 LESTER, Richard A. "Currency Issues to Overcome Depressions in Pennsylvania, 1723 and 1729." *J Pol Econ,* XLVI (1938), 324-375; XLVII (1939), 182-217.

16 LESTER, Richard A. *Monetary Experiments, Early American and Recent Scandinavian.* Princeton, 1939.

17 NETTELS, Curtis P. "The Beginnings of Money in Connecticut." *Trans Wis Acad Sci,* XXIII (1927), 1-28.

18 NETTELS, Curtis P. "The Origins of Paper Money in the English Colonies." *Econ Hist,* III (1934), 35-56.

19 RIDDELL, William R. "Benjamin Franklin and Colonial Money." *Pa Mag Hist,* LIV (1930), 52-64.

20 THAYER, Theodore G. "The Land-Bank System in the American Colonies." *J Econ Hist,* XIII (1953), 145-159.

British Regulations of Colonial Paper Currency

21 ERNST, Joseph A. "Genesis of the Currency Act of 1764: Virginia Paper Money and the Protection of British Investments." *Wm Mar Q,* 3rd ser., XXII (1965), 33-74.

Coins and Coinage

1 CHAPMAN, Henry. "The Colonial Coins of America Prior to the Declaration of Independence." *Numis,* LXI (1948), 75-87.

2 OGG, Frederick A. "Coins and Coinage in the New England Colonies." *N Eng Mag,* XXXIV (1903), 739-751.

Counterfeiting

3 SCOTT, Kenneth. *Counterfeiting in Colonial America.* New York, 1957.

THE ORGANIZATION OF SOCIETY

Social Structure

General

4 BRIDENBAUGH, Carl. *Myths and Realities.* See **42**.5.

5 MAIN, Jackson Turner. *The Social Structure of Revolutionary America.* Princeton, 1965.

Settled Areas

6 BAILYN, Bernard. "The Beekmans of New York: Trade, Politics, and Families." See **60**.10.

7 BAILYN, Bernard. *The New England Merchants.* See **54**.11.

8 DOLL, Eugene. "Social and Economic Organization in Two Pennsylvania German Religious Communities." *Am J Socio,* LVII (1951), 168-177.

9 EVANS, Emory G. "The Rise and Decline of the Virginia Aristocracy in the Eighteenth Century: The Nelsons." In *The Old Dominion,* ed. Darrett B. Rutman. Charlottesville, Va., 1964.

10 HENRETTA, James A. "Economic Development and Social Structure in Colonial Boston." *Wm Mar Q,* 3rd ser., XXII (1965), 75-92.

11 HIGH, James. "The Origins of Maryland's Middle-class in the Colonial Aristocractic Pattern." *Md Hist Mag,* LVII (1962), 334-345.

12 KENNEY, Alice P. "Dutch Patricians in Colonial Albany." *N Y Hist,* XLIX (1968), 249-283.

13 LAND, Aubrey C. "Economic Base and Social Structure: The Northern Chesapeake in the Eighteenth Century." *J Econ Hist,* XXV (1965), 639-654.

14 LEMON, James T. and Gary B. NASH. "The Distribution of Wealth in Eighteenth-Century America: A Century of Changes in Chester County, Pennsylvania, 1693-1802." *J Soc Hist,* II (1968), 1-24.

15 MARK, Irving. *Agrarian Conflicts in Colonial New York.* See **50**.13.

16 SCHONFELD, Robert G. and Spencer WILSON. "The Value of Personal Estates in Maryland, 1700-1710." *Md Hist Mag,* LVIII (1963), 333-343.

17 TOLLES, Frederick B. *Meeting House and Counting House.* See **34**.1.

18 TOLLES, Frederick B. "Town House and Country House Inventories from the Estate of William Logan, 1776." *Pa Mag Hist,* LXXXII (1958), 397-410.

19 WRIGHT, Louis B. *The First Gentleman of Virginia; Intellectual Qualities of the Early Colonial Ruling Class.* San Marino, Calif., 1940.

Frontier Areas

1 ABERNETHY, Thomas P. *Three Virginia Frontiers.* Baton Rouge, La., 1940.

2 LEACH, Douglas E. *The Northern Colonial Frontier, 1607-1763.* See **19.**8.

3 RAMSEY, Robert. *Carolina Cradle: Settlement of the Northwest Carolina Frontier, 1747-1762.* Chapel Hill, 1964.

4 SHIPTON, Clifford K. "The New England Frontier." *N Eng Q,* X (1937), 25-36.

5 TURNER, Frederick Jackson. "The Old West." *Proc Wis Hist Soc,* LVI (1909), 184-233.

Social Mobility

6 CRARY, Catherine S. "The American Dream: John Tabor Kempe's Rise from Poverty to Riches." *Wm Mar Q,* 3rd ser., XIV (1957), 176-195.

7 CRARY, Catherine S. "The Humble Immigrant and the American Dream: Some Case Histories, 1746-1776." *Miss Val Hist Rev,* XLVI (1959), 46-66.

8 HANDLIN, Oscar and Mary. "Ethnic Factors in Social Mobility." *Explor Entrep Hist,* IX (1956), 1-7.

9 LAND, Aubrey C. "Genesis of a Colonial Fortune: Daniel Dulany of Maryland." *Wm Mar Q,* 3rd ser., VII (1950), 255-269.

10 TEMPLE, Sarah B. and Kenneth COLEMAN. *Georgia Journeys: Being an Account of the Lives of Georgia's Original Settlers . . . 1732 until . . . 1754.* Athens, Ga., 1961.

Indebtedness

11 COLEMAN, Peter J. "The Insolvent Debtor in Rhode Island, 1745-1828." *Wm Mar Q,* 3rd ser., XXII (1965), 413-434.

12 FEER, Robert A. "Imprisonment for Debt in Massachusetts before 1800." *Miss Val Hist Rev,* XLVIII (1961), 252-269.

13 RANDALL, Edwin T. "Imprisonment for Debt in America: Fact and Fiction." *Miss Val Hist Rev,* XXXIX (1952), 89-102.

Poverty

14 DEUTSCH, Albert. "The Sick Poor in Colonial Times." *Am Hist Rev,* XLVI (1941), 560-579.

15 HEFFNER, William C. *History of Poor Relief Legislation in Pennsylvania, 1682-1913.* Cleona, Pa., 1913.

16 JERNEGAN, Marcus W. "The Development of Poor Relief in Colonial Virginia." *Soc Ser Rev,* III (1929), 1-19.

17 KELSO, Robert W. *History of Public Poor Relief in Massachusetts, 1620-1920.* Boston, 1922.

18 KLEBANER, Benjamin J. "Some Aspects of North Carolina Public Poor Relief, 1700-1860." *N C Hist Rev,* 31 (1954), 479-492.

19 MC ENTEGART, Bryan J. "How Seventeenth Century New York Cared for its Poor." *Thought,* I (1927), 588-612; II (1927), 403-429.

20 MACKEY, Howard. "The Operation of the English Old Poor Law in Colonial Virginia." *Va Mag Hist,* LXXIII (1965), 29-40.

1 MACKEY, Howard. "Social Welfare in Colonial Virginia: The Importance of the Old Poor Law." *Hist Mag P E Ch,* XXXVI (1967), 359-382.

2 STANTON, Martin W. *History of Public Poor Relief in New Jersey, 1609-1934.* New York, 1934.

THE STRUCTURE OF VALUES

The Promises and Problems of Abundance

General

3 JONES, Howard M. *O Strange New World. American Culture: The Formative Years.* New York, 1964.†

4 LEFLER, Hugh T. "Promotional Literature of the Southern Colonies." *J S Hist,* XXXIII (1967), 3-25.

5 MARX, Leo. *Machine in the Garden: Technology and the Pastoral Ideal in America.* New York, 1964.†

6 POTTER, David. *People of Plenty: Economic Abundance and the American Character.* Chicago, 1958.†

7 TUVESON, Ernest Lee. *Redeemer Nation: The Idea of America's Millennial Role.* Chicago, 1968.

8 WRIGHT, Louis B. *The Dream of Prosperity in Colonial America.* New York, 1965.

Utopian Experiments

9 CRANE, Verner W. "A Lost Utopia of the First American Frontier." *Sew Rev,* XXVII (1919), 46-81.

10 GOLLIN, Gillian L. *Moravians in Two Worlds.* New York, 1967.

11 LOOSE, Jack W. *A Study of Two Distinct Periods of Ephrata Cloister History.* Lancaster, Pa., 1951.

12 VOIGT, Gilbert P. "Ebenezer, Georgia: An Eighteenth Century Utopia." *Ga Rev,* IX (1955), 209-215.

Social Values

General

13 ANDREWS, Charles M. *Colonial Folkways: a Chronicle of American Life in the Reign of the Georges.* New Haven, 1919.

14 BEATTY, Edward C. *William Penn as Social Philosopher.* New York, 1939.

15 BRIGHAM, Clarence S. *An Account of American Almanacs and Their Value for Historical Study.* Worcester, Mass., 1925.

16 BROCK, Peter. *Pacifism in the United States from the Colonial Era to the First World War.* Princeton, 1968.

17 DIAMOND, Sigmund. "Values as an Obstacle to Economic Growth: The American Colonies." *J Econ Hist,* XXVII (1967), 561-575.

18 LABAREE, Leonard W. *Conservatism in Early American History.* New York, 1948.†

1 LANGDON, William C. *Everyday Things in American Life 1607-1776.* New York, 1937.

2 MORGAN, Edmund S. "The Puritan Ethic and the American Revolution." *Wm Mar Q,* 3rd ser., XXIV (1967), 3-43.

3 WECTOR, Dixon. *The Saga of American Society; A Record of Social Aspiration, 1607-1937.* New York, 1937.

4 WOODWARD, C. Vann. "The Southern Ethic in a Puritan World." *Wm Mar Q,* 3rd ser., XXV (1968), 343-370.

Work, Striving, and Acquisitiveness

5 AIKEN, John R. "Benjamin Franklin, Karl Marx, and the Labor Theory of Value." *Pa Mag Hist,* XC (1966), 378-422.

6 BERTELSON, David. *The Lazy South.* New York, 1967.

7 DORFMAN, Joseph. *The Economic Mind in American Civilization, 1606-1865.* 2 vols. New York, 1946.

8 GALLACHER, Stuart A. "Franklin's *Way to Wealth:* A Florilegium of Proverbs and Wise Sayings." *J Eng Ger Philol,* XLVIII (1949), 229-251.

9 HAYWOOD, C. Robert. "The Influence of Mercantilism on Social Attitudes in the South, 1700-1763." *J Hist Ideas,* XX (1959), 577-586.

10 HAYWOOD, C. Robert. "The Mind of the North Carolina Advocates of Mercantilism." *N C Hist Rev,* XXXIII (1955), 139-165

11 JOHNSON, Edgar A. J. *American Economic Thought in the Seventeenth Century.* London, 1932.

12 TOLLES, Frederick B. *Meeting House and Counting House.* See **30.11.**

Status and Hierarchy

13 COLE, Arthur H. "The Social Significance of New England Idiomatic Phrases." *Proc Am Ant Soc,* LXX (1960), 21-68.

14 DAWES, Norman H. "Titles as Symbols of Prestige in Seventeenth-Century New England." *Wm Mar Q,* 3rd ser., VI (1949), 69-83.

15 GREENE, Evarts B. "The Code of Honor in Colonial and Revolutionary Times, with Special Reference to New England." *Pub Col Soc Mass,* XXVI (1927), 367-388.

16 HEMPHILL, John M., ed. "John Wayles Rates His Neighbors." *Va Mag Hist,* LXVI (1958), 302-306.

17 KROUT, John A. "Behind the Coat of Arms; A Phase of Prestige in Colonial New York." *N Y Hist,* XVI (1935), 45-52.

18 MORISON, Samuel E. "Precedence at Harvard College in the Seventeenth Century." *Proc Am Ant Soc,* XLII (1933), 371-431.

19 SHIPTON, Clifford K. "Ye Mystery of Ye Ages Solved, or, How Placing Worked at Colonial Harvard and Yale." *Har Alum Bull,* LVII (1954-1955), 258-259,262-263 (cf 417).

Race

20 JORDAN, Winthrop D. "American Chiaroscuro: The Status and Definition of Mulattoes in the British Colonies." *Wm Mar Q,* 3rd ser., XIX (1962), 183-200.

1 JORDAN, Winthrop D. *White Over Black: The Development of American Attitudes Toward the Negro, 1550-1812.* Chapel Hill, 1968.

2 MIDDLETON, Arthur P. "The Strange Story of Jobo Ben Solomon." *Wm Mar Q,* 3rd ser., V (1948), 342-350.

3 MOORE, Wilbert E. "Slave Law and the Social Structure." *J Neg Hist,* XXVI (1941), 171-202.

Perils of the Wilderness

4 HEIMERT, Alan. "Puritanism, the Wilderness, and the Frontier." *N Eng Q,* XXVI (1953), 361-382.

5 WRIGHT, Louis B. *Culture on the Moving Frontier.* Bloomington, Ind., 1955.†

Perils of Prosperity and Secularization

6 BUSHMAN, Richard L. *From Puritan to Yankee.* See **34**.5.

7 COLMAN, Benjamin. "Letter of Rev. Benjamin Colman to the Wife of John George of Boston who had Sought his Advice as to her Scruples About the Richness of her Fashionable Apparel, 17 February 1700-01." *Pub Col Soc Mass,* VIII (1906), 247-250.

8 EZELL, John S. *Fortune's Merry Wheel: Lottery in America.* Cambridge, Mass., 1960.

9 GRISWOLD, A. Whitney. "Three Puritans on Prosperity." *N Eng Q,* VII (1934), 475-493.

10 MILLER, Perry. *The New England Mind: Colony to Province.* Cambridge, Mass., 1961.†

11 MORGAN, Edmund S. "Puritan Hostility to the Theatre." *Proc Am Philos Soc,* CX (1966), 340-347.

12 PARKES, Henry B. "Morals and Law Enforcement in Colonial New England." *N Eng Q,* V (1932), 431-452.

13 PARKES, Henry B. "Sexual Morals and the Great Awakening." *N Eng Q,* III (1930), 133-135.

14 SEAVER, Henry L. "Hair and Holiness." *Proc Mass Hist Soc,* LXVIII (1952), 3-20.

15 TOLLES, Frederick B. *Meeting House and Counting House.* See **34**.1.

Death

16 FALES, Martha G. "The Early American Way of Death." *Essex Inst Hist Coll,* C (1964), 75-84.

17 NEEDHAM, A. C. "Random Notes on Funeral Rings, Compiled from Various Sources." *Old-Time N Eng,* XXXIX (1949), 93-97.

18 WOOD, R. C. "Life, Death and Poetry as seen by the Pennsylvania Dutch." *Monat,* XXXVII (1945), 453-465.

Social Deviation

General

19 ERIKSON, Kai T. *Wayward Puritans. A Study in the Sociology of Deviance.* New York, 1966.

Crime and Punishments

1 FITZROY, Herbert William. "The Punishment of Crime in Provincial Pennsylvania." *Pa Mag Hist,* LX (1936), 242-269.

2 GIPSON, Lawrence H. *Crime and Its Punishment in Provincial Pennsylvania; A Phase of the Social History of the Commonwealth.* Bethlehem, Pa., 1935.

3 SEMMES, Raphael. *Crime and Punishment in Early Maryland.* Baltimore, 1938.

Witchcraft

4 BURR, George L. "New England's Place in the History of Witchcraft." *Proc Am Ant Soc,* XXI (1911), 185-217.

5 KITTREDGE, George Lyman. *Witchcraft in Old and New England.* Cambridge, Mass., 1929.

6 PROPER, David R. "Salem Witchcraft, A Brief History." *Essex Inst Hist Coll,* CII (1966), 213-223.

7 RIDDELL, William R. "William Penn and Witchcraft." *J Crim Law,* XVIII (1927), 11-16.

8 RIDDELL, William R. "Witchcraft in Old New York." *J Crim Law,* XIX (1928), 252-258.

9 ROBBINS, Fred Gibson. "Witchcraft." *Essex Inst Hist Coll,* LXV (1929), 209-239.

10 STARKEY, Marion L. *The Devil in Massachusetts: A Modern Inquiry into the Salem Witch Trials.* New York, 1949.†

Suicide and Mental Illness

11 DEUTSCH, Albert. *The Mentally Ill in America: A History of their Care and Treatment from Colonial Times.* New York, 1946.

12 NOBLE, John. *A Glance at Suicide as Dealt with in the Colony and in the Province of the Massachusetts Bay.* Cambridge, Mass., 1903.

Standards and Styles of Living
For additional references see the general section on Culture.

Cultural Provincialism

13 BRIDENBAUGH, Carl. *Myths and Realities.* See **42.5**.

14 BYRD, William. *Another Secret Diary of William Byrd of Westover, 1739-1741, with Letters and Literary Exercises, 1696-1726.* Richmond, 1942.

15 BYRD, William. *The Prose Works of William Byrd of Westover: Narratives of a Colonial Virginian.* Cambridge, Mass., 1966.

16 BYRD, William. *The Secret Diary of William Byrd of Westover, 1709-1712.* Richmond, 1941.

17 BYRD, William. *William Byrd of Virginia: The London Diary (1717-1721) and other Writings.* New York, 1958.

18 CADY, Edwin H. *The Gentleman in America: A Literary Study in American Culture.* Syracuse, N.Y., 1949.

19 CARTER, Landon. *The Diary of Colonel Landon Carter of Sabine Hall, 1752-1778.* 2 vols. Charlottesville, Va., 1965.

20 CLIVE, John and Bernard BAILYN. "England's Cultural Provinces: Scotland and America." *Wm Mar Q,* 3rd ser., XI (1954), 200-213.

21 CONNELY, Willard. "Colonial Americans in Oxford and Cambridge." *Am Ox,* XXIX (1942), 6-17.

1 CONNELY, Willard. "List of Colonial Americans in Oxford and Cambridge." *Am Ox,* XXIX (1942), 75-77.

2 GRIFFITH, Lucille. "English Education for Virginia Youth." *Va Mag Hist,* LXXIX (1961), 7-27.

3 HOMANS, George C. "The Puritans and the Clothing Industry in England." *N Eng Q,* XIII (1940), 519-529.

4 INGRAM, K. E. "The West India Trade of an English Furniture Firm in the 18th Century." *Jam Hist Rev,* III (1962), no. 3, 22-37.

5 KLEIN, Milton M. "The Cultural Tyros of Colonial New York." *S Atl Q,* LXVI (1967), 218-232.

6 KRAUS, Michael. *The Atlantic Civilization: Eighteenth-Century Origins.* Ithaca, 1949.†

7 LIVINGSTON, William, and others. *The Independent Reflector or Weekly Essays on Sundry Important Subjects more Particularly Adapted to the Province of New York.* Cambridge, Mass., 1963.

8 LYNN, Kenneth S. *Mark Twain and Southwestern Humor.* Boston, 1959. (Chapter I describes the provincialism of William Byrd II.)

9 READ, Conyers. "The English Elements in Benjamin Franklin." *Pa Mag Hist,* LXIV (1840), 314-330.

10 SACHSE, William L. *The Colonial American in Britain.* Madison, Wis., 1956.

11 SHERIDAN, Richard. "Planter and Historian: The Career of William Beckford of Jamaica and England, 1744-1799." *Jam Hist Rev,* IV (1964), 36-59.

12 SWAN, Mabel M. "Where Elias Hasket Derby Bought his Furniture." *Antiques,* XX (1931), 280-282.

13 TOLLES, Frederick B. *Quakers and the Atlantic Culture.* New York, 1960.

14 WALLACE, Wesley H. "Cultural and Social Advertising in Early North Carolina Newspapers." *N C Hist Rev,* 281-309.

15 WATSON, Alan D. "Ordinaries in Colonial Eastern North Carolina." *N C Hist Rev,* XLV (1968), 67-83.

16 WRIGHT, Louis B. *The First Gentlemen of Virginia.* See **72**.19.

Development of Urban Culture

17 BOWES, Frederick P. *The Culture of Early Charleston.* Chapel Hill, 1942.

18 BRIDENBAUGH, Carl. *Cities in Revolt.* See **48**.13.

19 BRIDENBAUGH, Carl. *Cities in the Wilderness.* See **48**.14.

20 BRIDENBAUGH, Carl. "The High Cost of Living in Boston, 1728." *N Eng Q,* V (1932), 800-811.

21 BRIDENBAUGH, Carl and Jessica. *Rebels and Gentlemen: Philadelphia in the Age of Franklin.* New York, 1942.†

22 SINGLETON, Esther. *Social New York under the Georges 1714-1776; Houses, Streets, and Country Homes, with Chapters on Fashions, Furniture, China, Plate and Manners. . . .* New York, 1902.

Philanthropy

1 KELLEN, William V. "William Price, a Colonial Philanthropist." *Proc Mass Hist Soc,* LXV (1940), 511-517.

The Americanization of Society: Communications and Homogenization

General

2 KRAUS, Michael. *Intercolonial Aspects of American Culture on the Eve of the Revolution, with Special Reference to the Northern Towns.* New York, 1928.

The Post Office

3 BUTLER, Ruth L. *Doctor Franklin, Postmaster General.* Garden City, N.Y., 1928.

4 SMITH, William. *The History of the Post Office in British North America, 1639-1870.*

Travel and Transportation

5 ANDREWS, Charles M. *Colonial Folkways.* See **74**.13.

6 BRIDENBAUGH, Carl. "Colonial Newport as a Summer Resort. *R I Hist Soc Coll,* XXVI (1933), 1-23.

7 BRIDENBAUGH, Carl. "Baths and Watering Places of Colonial America." *Wm Mar Q,* 3rd ser., III (1946), 151-181.

8 CLONTS, F. W. "Travel and Transportation in Colonial North Carolina." *N C Hist Rev,* III (1926), 16-35.

9 HAMILTON, Alexander. *Gentleman's Progress: The Itinerarium of Dr. Alexander Hamilton, 1744.* Ed. Carl Bridenbaugh. Chapel Hill, 1948.

10 LANE, Wheaton J. *From Indian Trail to Iron Horse. Travel and Transportation in New Jersey, 1620-1860.* Princeton, 1939.

11 MERENESS, Newton D., ed. *Travels in the American Colonies.* See **1**.15.

12 RYAN, Frank W., Jr. "Travelers in South Carolina in the Eighteenth Century." *Yr Bk Charleston S C,* 1945 (1948), 184-256.

Development of Common Values

13 DICKINSON, John. "A Pennsylvania Farmer at the Court of King George: John Dickinson's London Letters, 1754-1756." *Pa Mag Hist,* LXXXVI (1962), 241-287, 417-453.

14 HARKNESS, Albert, Jr. "Americanism and Jenkins' Ear." *Miss Val Hist Rev,* XXXVII (1950), 61-90.

15 KOEBNER, Richard. *Empire.* See **12**.3.

16 MERRITT, Richard L. *Symbols of American Community, 1735-1775.* New Haven, 1966.

17 MILLER, Ralph N. "American Nationalism as a Theory of Nature." *Wm Mar Q,* 3rd ser., XII (1955), 74-95.

18 SAVELLE, Max. "The Appearance of an American Attitude Toward External Affairs, 1750-1775." *Am Hist Rev,* LII (1947), 655-666.

19 VARG, Paul. "The Advent of Nationalism, 1758-1776." *Am Q,* XVI (1964), 160-181.

The Internalization of Values

1 BAILYN, Bernard. "Butterfield's Adams: Notes for a Sketch." *Wm Mar Q*, 3rd ser., XIX (1962), 238-256.

2 BUSHMAN, Richard L. "On the Uses of Psychology: Conflict and Conciliation in Benjamin Franklin." *Hist Theory,* V (1966), 225-240.

3 GREENE, Jack P. *Landon Carter: An Inquiry into the Personal Values and Social Imperatives of the Eighteenth-Century Virginia Gentry.* Charlottesville, Va., 1965.†

4 SEWALL, Samuel E. *Diary, 1674-1729. Coll Mass Hist Soc,* 5th ser., V-VII (1878-1882).

THE AGENCIES OF ENFORCEMENT

The Family

General

5 CALHOUN, Arthur W. *A Social History of the American Family from Colonial Times to the Present.* 3 vols. Cleveland, 1917-1919.

6 MORGAN, Edmund S. *The Puritan Family: Religion and Domestic Relations in Seventeenth Century New England.* Rev. and enlarged. New York, 1966.†

7 MORGAN, Edmund S. *Virginians at Home: Family Life in the Eighteenth Century.* Williamsburg, Va., 1952.†

8 ROTHMAN, David J. "A Note on the Study of the Colonial Family." *Wm Mar Q,* 3rd ser., XXIII (1966), 627-634.

Role of Women

9 BENSON, Mary S. *Women in Eighteenth-Century America; A Study of Opinion and Social Usage.* New York, 1935.

10 COBBLEDICK, M. Robert. "The Property Rights of Women in Puritan New England." *Studies in the Science of Society. . . .* Ed. George P. Murdock. New Haven, 1937.

11 DEXTER, Elisabeth A. *Colonial Women of Affairs; Women in Business and the Professions in America before 1776.* 2nd ed., rev. Boston, 1931.

12 DOUGLAS, James. *The Status of Women in New England and New France.* Kingston, Ont., 1912.

13 SPRUILL, Julia Cherry. *Women's Life and Work in the Southern Colonies.* Chapel Hill, 1938.

Marriage Customs

14 DOTEN, Dana. *The Art of Bundling. . . .* New York, 1938.

15 ROTHENBERG, Charles. "Marriage, Morals and the Law in Colonial America. *N Y Law Rev,* LXXIV (1940), 393-398.

1 STEVENSON, Noel C. "Marital Rights in the Colonial Period." *N Eng Hist Geneal Reg,* CIX (1955), 84-90.

2 STILES, Henry R. *Bundling ... its Origin, Progress and Decline in America.* (1st ed., 1869.) New York, 1931.

Childrearing Patterns

3 BUCKINGHAM, Clyde E. "Early American Orphanages: Ebenezer and Bethesda." *Soc Forces,* XXVI (1948), 311-321.

4 CALEY, Percy B. "Child Life in Colonial Western Pennsylvania." *W Pa Hist Mag,* IX (1926), 33-49, 104-121, 188-201, 256-275.

5 EARLE, Alice M. *Child Life in Colonial Days.* New York, 1899.

6 FLEMING, Sandford. *Children and Puritanism, the Place of Children in the Life and Thought of New England Churches, 1620-1847.* New Haven, 1933.

7 KIEFER, Monica M. *American Children Through Their Books, 1700-1835.* Philadelphia, 1948.

8 KIEFER, Monica M. "Early American Childhood in the Middle Atlantic Area." *Pa Mag Hist,* LXVIII (1944), 3-37.

9 O'BRIEN, Edward J. *Child Welfare Legislation in Maryland, 1634-1936.* Washington, D.C., 1937.

10 SCHLESINGER, Elizabeth B. "Cotton Mather and his Children." *Wm Mar Q,* 3rd ser., X (1953), 181-189

11 SURRENCY, Erwin C. "Whitefield, Habersham, and the Bethesda Orphanage." *Ga Hist Q,* XXXIV (1950), 87-105.

Formal Education

General

12 BAILYN, Bernard. *Education in the Forming of American Society: Needs and Opportunities for Study.* Chapel Hill, 1960.

Missions

13 ALLEN, W. O. B. and Edmund MC CLURE. *Two Hundred Years: The History of the Society for Promoting Christian Knowledge, 1698-1898.* London, 1898.

14 BULTMANN, William A. and Phyllis W. "The Roots of American Humanitarianism: A Study of the Membership of the S.P.C.K. and the S.P.G., 1699-1720." *Hist Mag P E Ch,* XXXIII (1964), 3-48.

15 CATIR, Norman J., Jr. "Berkeley's Successful Failure: A Study of George Berkeley's Contribution to American Education." *Hist Mag P E Ch,* XXXIII (1964), 65-82.

16 COWIE, Leonard W. *Henry Newman (1670-1743), An American in London, 1708-1743.* London, 1956.

17 GOODWIN, Mary F. "Christianizing and Educating the Negro in Colonial Virginia." *Hist Mag P E Ch,* I (1932), 143-152.

18 GRAY, Elma E. and Leslie R. *Wilderness Christians. The Moravian Mission to the Delaware Indians.* Ithaca, 1956.

19 JERNEGAN, Marcus W. "Slavery and Conversion in the American Colonies." *Am Hist Rev,* XXI (1916), 504-527.

20 JONES, Jerome W. "The Established Virginia Church and the Conversion of Negroes and Indians, 1620-1760." *J Neg Hist,* XLVI (1961), 12-23.

1 KELLAWAY, William. *The New England Company 1649-1776: Missionary Society to the American Indians.* New York, 1962.

2 KEMP, William W. *The Support of Schools in Colonial New York by the Society for the Propagation of the Gospel in Foreign Parts.* New York, 1913.

3 KLINGBERG, Frank J. "The African Immigrant in Colonial Pennsylvania and Delaware. *Hist Mag P E Ch,* XI (1942), 126-153.

4 KLINGBERG, Frank J. *Anglican Humanitarianism in Colonial New York.* Philadelphia, 1940.

5 KLINGBERG, Frank J. *An Appraisal of the Negro in Colonial South Carolina.* Washington, D.C., 1941.

6 MC CULLOCH, Samuel C., ed. *British Humanitarianism: Essays Honoring Frank J. Klingberg.* Philadelphia, 1950.

7 MC CULLOCH, Samuel C. "The Foundation and Early Work of the Society for Promoting Christian Knowledge." *Hist Mag P E Ch,* XVIII (1949), 3-22.

8 MC CULLOCH, Samuel C. "The Foundation and Early Work of the Society for the Propagation of the Gospel in Foreign Parts." *Hist Mag P E Ch,* XX (1951), 121-135.

9 MC HUGH, Thomas F. "The Moravian Mission to the American Indian: Early American Peace Corps." *Pa Hist,* XXXIII (1966), 412-431.

10 PASCOE, C. F. *Two Hundred Years of the S.P.G.* 2 vols. London, 1901.

11 PENNINGTON, Edgar L. *The Reverend Thomas Bray.* Philadelphia, 1934.

12 PIERRE, C. E. "The Work of the Society for the Propagation of the Gospel in Foreign Parts among the Negroes in the Colonies." *J Neg Hist,* I (1916), 349-360.

13 PILCHER, George W. "Samuel Davies and the Instruction of Negroes in Virginia." *Va Mag Hist,* LXXIV (1966), 293-300.

14 ROBINSON, W. Stitt. "Indian Education and Missions in Colonial Virginia." *J S Hist,* XVIII (1952), 152-168.

15 THOMPSON, Henry P. *Into All Lands: The History of the Society for the Propagation of the Gospel in Foreign Parts, 1701-1950.* London, 1951.

16 THOMPSON, Henry P. *Thomas Bray.* London, 1954.

17 VIBERT, Faith. "The Society for the Propagation of the Gospel in Foreign Parts. Its Work for the Negroes in North America before 1783." *J Neg Hist,* XVIII (1933), 171-212.

Schools

18 BELL, Whitfield J., Jr. "Benjamin Franklin and the German Charity Schools." *Proc Am Philos Soc,* XCIX (1955), 381-387.

19 BROOKES, George S. *Friend Anthony Benezet.* Philadelphia, 1937.

20 JACKSON, Joseph. "A Philadelphia Schoolmaster of the Eighteenth Century." *Pa Mag Hist,* XXV (1911), 315-332.

21 JERNEGAN, Marcus W. "The Educational Development of the Southern Colonies." *School Rev,* XXVII (1919), 360-376, 405-425.

1 KILPATRICK, William H. *The Dutch Schools of New Netherland and Colonial New York.* Washington, D.C., 1912.

2 LIVINGWOOD, Frederick G. *Eighteenth Century Reformed Schools.* Norristown, Pa., 1930.

3 MC ANEAR, Beverly. "The Charter of the Academy of Newark." *Del Hist,* IV (1950), 149-156.

4 MC CAUL, Robert L. "Education in Georgia during the Period of Royal Government, 1752-1776." *Ga Hist Q,* XL (1956), 103-112, 248-259.

5 MARTIN, George H. *The Evolution of the Massachusetts Public School System: A Historical Sketch.* New York, 1894.

6 MAURER, Charles L. *Early Lutheran Education in Pennsylvania.* Philadelphia, 1932. *Proc Pa-Ger Soc,* XL (1929).

7 MIDDLEKAUFF, Robert. *Ancients and Axioms: Secondary Education in Eighteenth-Century New England.* New Haven, 1963.

8 MORGAN, George. "The Colonial Origin of Newark Academy and of Other Classical Schools from which Arose Many Colleges and Universities." *Del Note,* VII (1934), 7-30.

9 MURDOCK, Kenneth B. "The Teaching of Latin and Greek at the Boston Latin School in 1712." *Pub Col Soc Mass,* XXVII (1932), 21-29.

10 PEARS, Thomas C., Jr. "Colonial Education among Presbyterians." *J Presby Hist Soc,* XXX (1952), 115-126, 165-174.

11 SEYBOLT, Robert F. *The Public Schoolmasters of Colonial Boston.* Cambridge, Mass., 1939.

12 SEYBOLT, Robert F. *The Public Schools of Colonial Boston, 1635-1775.* Cambridge, Mass., 1935.

13 SHIPTON, Clifford K. "Secondary Education in the Puritan Colonies." *N Eng Q,* VII (1934), 646-661.

14 SMALL, Walter H. *Early New England Schools.* Boston, 1914.

15 STANDER, Golda G. "Jesuit Educational Institutions in the City of New York (1683-1860)." *U S Cath Hist Rec,* XXIV (1934), 209-275.

16 STRAUB, Jean S. "Teaching in the Friend's Latin School of Philadelphia in the Eighteenth Century." *Pa Mag Hist,* XCI (1967), 436-456.

17 WEAVER, Glenn. "Benjamin Franklin and the Pennsylvania Germans." *Wm Mar Q,* 3rd ser., XIV (1957), 536-559.

18 WEBER, Samuel E. *The Charity School Movement in Colonial Pennsylvania.* Philadelphia, 1905.

19 WELLS, Guy F. *Parish Education in Colonial Virginia.* New York, 1923.

20 WOODY, Thomas. *Early Quaker Education in Pennsylvania.* New York, 1920.

21 WOODY, Thomas. *A History of Women's Education in the United States.* 2 vols. New York, 1929.

Apprenticeship

22 JERNEGAN, Marcus W. *Laboring and Dependent Classes.* See **67**.14.

23 SEYBOLT, Robert F. *Apprenticeship & Apprenticeship Education in Colonial New England & New York.* New York, 1917.

1 SEYBOLT, Robert F. *The Evening School in Colonial America.* Urbana, Ill., 1925.

Higher Education

2 ADAMS, Herbert B. *The College of William and Mary.* Washington, D.C., 1887.

3 BRODERICK, Francis L. "Pulpit, Physics, and Politics: The Curriculum of the College of New Jersey, 1746-1794." *Wm Mar Q,* 3rd ser., VI (1949), 42-68.

4 CHEYNEY, Edward P. *History of the University of Pennsylvania, 1740-1940.* Philadelphia, 1940.

5 COLLINS, Varnum L. *President Witherspoon, 1723-1794.* 2 vols. Princeton, 1925.

6 COME, Donald R. "The Influence of Princeton on Higher Education in the South before 1825." *Wm Mar Q,* 3rd ser., II (1945), 352-396.

7 COWIE, Alexander. *Educational Problems at Yale College in the Eighteenth Century.* (Tercentenary Pamphlet Series LV). New Haven, 1936.

8 FOSTER, Margery S. *"Out of Smalle Beginnings . . .": An Economic History of Harvard College in the Puritan Period (1636-1712).* Cambridge, Mass., 1962.

9 HOFSTADTER, Richard and Walter P. METZGER. *The Development of Academic Freedom in the United States.* New York, 1955.

10 INGRAM, George H. "The Story of the Log College." *J Presby Hist Soc,* XII (1927), 487-511.

11 INGRAM, George H. "William Tennent, Sr., the Founder, 1673-1746." *J Presby Hist Soc,* XIV (1930), 1-27.

12 LANGSTAFF, John B. "Anglican Origins of Columbia University." *Hist Mag P E Ch,* IX (1940), 257-260.

13 MC ANEAR, Beverly. "College Founding in the American Colonies, 1745-1775." *Miss Val Hist Rev,* XLII (1955), 24-44.

14 MC ANEAR, Beverly. "The Raising of Funds by the Colonial Colleges." *Miss Val Hist Rev,* XXXVIII (1952), 591-612.

15 MC ANEAR, Beverly. "The Selection of an Alma Mater by Pre-Revolutionary Students." *Pa Mag Hist,* LXXIII (1949), 429-440.

16 MC CALLUM, James D. *Eleazar Wheelock, Founder of Dartmouth College.* Hanover, N.H., 1939.

17 MC CAUL, Robert L. "Whitefield's Bethesda College Projects and Other Major Attempts to Found Colonial Colleges." *Ga Hist Q,* XLIV (1960), 263-277.

18 MC KEEHAN, Louis W. *Yale Science: The First Hundred Years, 1701-1801.* New York, 1947.

19 MIDDLETON, Arthur P. "Anglican Contributions to Higher Education in Colonial America." *Pa Hist,* XXV (1958), 251-268.

20 MORGAN, Edmund S. *The Gentle Puritan: A Life of Ezra Stiles, 1727-1795.* New Haven, 1962.

21 MORISON, Samuel E. *Three Centuries of Harvard. 1636-1936.* Cambridge, Mass., 1936.

1 OVIATT, Edwin. *The Beginnings of Yale (1701-1726).* New Haven, 1916.

2 POTTER, Alfred C. "The Harvard College Library, 1723-1735." *Pub Col Soc Mass,* XXV (1924), 1-13.

3 POTTER, David. *Debating in the Colonial Chartered Colleges.* New York, 1944.

4 PRATT, Anne S. "The Books Sent from England by Jeremiah Dummer to Yale College." In *Papers in Honor of Andrew Keogh, Librarian of Yale University,* by the Staff of the Library. New Haven, 1938.

5 PRATT, Anne S. and Andrew KEOGH. "The Yale Library of 1742." *Yale U Lib Gaz,* XV (1940), 29-40.

6 ROBBINS, Caroline. "Library of Liberty—Assembled for Harvard College by Thomas Hollis of Lincoln's Inn." *Har Lib Bull,* V (1951), 5-23, 181-196.

7 SCHMIDT, George P. *Princeton and Rutgers: The Two Colonial Colleges of New Jersey.* Princeton, 1964.

8 SHORES, Louis. *Origins of the American College Library, 1638-1800.* Nashville, Tenn., 1934.

9 SMITH, P. Kingsley. "Samuel Johnson of Connecticut." *Ang Theol Rev,* XXXIX (1957), 217-229.

10 TEWKSBURY, Donald G. *The Founding of American Colleges and Universities before the Civil War, with Particular Reference to the Religious Influences Bearing on the College Movement,* New York, 1932.

11 TUCKER, Louis L. *Puritan Protagonist: President Thomas Clap of Yale College.* Chapel Hill, 1962.

12 TYLER, Lyon G. *The College of William and Mary in Virginia: Its History and Work. 1693-1907.* Richmond, Va., 1907.

13 WALSH, James J. *Education of the Founding Fathers of the Republic: Scholasticism in the Colonial Colleges; A Neglected Chapter in the History of American Education.* New York, 1935.

14 WERTENBAKER, Thomas J. *Princeton, 1746-1896.* Princeton, 1946.

15 WING, Donald G. and Margaret L. JOHNSON. "The Books Given by Elihu Yale in 1718." *Yale U Lib Gaz,* XIII (1939), 46-47.

16 YOUNG, Edward J. "Subjects for Master's Degree in Harvard College from 1655 to 1791." *Proc Mass Hist Soc,* XVIII (1880-1881), 119-151.

Libraries

Public and University Libraries

17 ABBOT, George M. *A Short History of the Library Company of Philadelphia.* Philadelphia, 1913.

18 EDMUNDS, Albert J. "The First Books Imported by America's First Great Library, 1732." *Pa Mag Hist,* XXX (1906), 300-308.

19 GRAY, Austin K. *Benjamin Franklin's Library: A Short Account of the Library Company of Philadelphia, 1731-1931.* New York, 1937.

1 KEEP, Austin B. *History of the New York Society Library, with an Introductory Chapter on Libraries in Colonial New York, 1698-1776.* New York, 1908.

2 KEEP, Austin B. *The Library in Colonial New York.* New York, 1909.

3 KORTY, Margaret B. *Benjamin Franklin and Eighteenth-Century American Libraries.* Philadelphia, 1965.

4 LAMBERTON, E. V. "Colonial Libraries of Pennsylvania." *Pa Mag Hist,* XLII (1918), 193-234.

5 *The New York Society Library, Founded in 1754; being a Brief Resume of its History, together with its Officers and Benefactors.* New York, 1937.

6 PENNINGTON, Edgar L. "The Beginnings of the Library in Charles Town, South Carolina." *Proc Am Ant Soc,* XLIV (1934), 159-187.

7 SHERA, Jesse H. *Foundations of the Public Library ... in New England, 1629-1855.* Chicago, 1949.

8 WHEELER, Joseph T. "Thomas Bray and the Maryland Parochial Libraries." *Md Hist Mag,* XXXIV (1939), 246-265.

9 WOLF, Edwin, II. "Franklin and his Friends Choose their Books." *Pa Mag Hist,* LXXX (1956), 11-36.

Private Libraries

10 BRAYTON, Susan S. "The Library of an Eighteenth-Century Gentleman of Rhode Island." *N Eng Q,* VIII (1935), 277-283.

11 ROBINSON, C. F. and Robin. "Three Early Massachusetts Libraries." *Pub Col Soc Mass,* XXVIII (1935), 107-175.

12 SMART, George K. "Private Libraries in Colonial Virginia." *Am Lit,* X (1938), 24-52.

13 TUTTLE, Julius H. "The Libraries of the Mathers." *Proc Am Ant Soc,* XX (1910), 269-356.

14 WEEKS, Stephen B. *Libraries and Literature in North Carolina in the 18th Century.* Washington, D.C., 1895.

15 WHEELER, Joseph T. "The Layman's Libraries and the Provincial Library." *Md Hist Mag,* XXV (1940), 60-73.

16 WOLF, Edwin, II. "The Library of a Philadelphia Judge, 1708." *Pa Mag Hist,* LXXXIII (1959), 180-191.

17 WOLF, Edwin, II. "The Library of Ralph Asheton: The Book Background of a Colonial Philadelphia Lawyer." *Pap Bibliog Soc Am,* LVIII (1964), 345-379.

18 WOLF, Edwin, II. "A Parcel of Books for the Province in 1700." *Pa Mag Hist,* LXXXIX (1965), 428-446.

19 WOLF, Edwin, II. "The Reconstruction of Benjamin Franklin's Library: An Unorthodox Jigsaw Puzzle." *Pap Bibliog Soc Am,* LVI (1962), 1-154.

20 WRIGHT, Louis B. "The 'Gentleman's Library' in Early Virginia: The Literary Interests of the First Carters." *Hunt Lib Q,* I (1937), 3-61.

The Press

Books and the Book Trade

21 BRIDENBAUGH, Carl. "The Press and the Book in Eighteenth Century Philadelphia." *Pa Mag Hist,* LXV (1941), 1-30.

1 FORD, Worthington C. *The Boston Book Market, 1679-1700.* Boston, 1917.

2 HARLAN, Robert D. "William Strahan's American Book Trade, 1744-1776." *Lib Q,* XXXI (1961), 235-244.

3 HERRICK, C. A. *The Early New-Englanders; What Did They Read?* London, 1918.

4 LEHMANN-HAUPT, Hellmut, Lawrence C. WROTH, and Rollo G. SILVER. *The Book in America: A History of the Making and Selling of Books in the United States.* 2nd ed. New York, 1951.

5 SLOANE, William. *Children's Books in England and America in the Seventeenth Century: A History and Checklist.* New York, 1955.

6 WEEKS, Stephen B. *The Press of North Carolina in the 18th Century; with Biographical Sketches of Printers, an Account of the Manufacture of Paper, and Bibliography of the Issues.* Brooklyn, N.Y., 1891.

7 WHEELER, Joseph T. "Books Owned by Marylanders, 1700-1776." *Md Hist Mag,* XXXV (1940), 337-353.

8 WHEELER, Joseph T. "Booksellers and Circulating Libraries in Colonial Maryland." *Md Hist Mag,* XXXIV (1939), 111-137.

9 WHEELER, Joseph T. "Reading Interests of the Professional Classes in Colonial Maryland, 1700-1776." *Md Hist Mag,* XXXVI (1941), 184-201, 281-301; XXXVII (1942), 26-41, 291-310; XXXVIII (1943), 37-55, 167-180.

10 WITTKE, Carl F. *The German-Language Press in America.* Lexington, Ky., 1957.

11 WROTH, Lawrence C. *An American Bookshelf, 1755.* Philadelphia, 1934.

12 WROTH, Lawrence C. *A History of Printing in Colonial Maryland, 1686-1776.* Baltimore, 1922.

13 WROTH, Lawrence C. *Typographic Heritage: Selected Essays.* New York, 1949.

Newspapers

14 BRIGHAM, Clarence. *History and Bibliography of American Newspapers.* See 1.4.

15 CARLSON, C. Lennart. "Samuel Keimer, a Study in the Transit of English Culture to Colonial Pennsylvania." *Pa Mag Hist,* LXI (1937), 357-386.

16 COHEN, Hennig. *The South Carolina Gazette, 1732-1775.* Columbia, S.C., 1953.

17 KOBRE, Sydney. *The Development of the Colonial Newspaper.* Pittsburgh, 1944.

Magazines

18 MOTT, Frank L. *American Journalism: A History, 1690-1960.* 3rd ed. New York, 1962.

19 MOTT, Frank L. *A History of American Magazines, 1741-1905.* Vol. I, 1741-1850. New York, 1930.

20 RICHARDSON, Lyon N. *A History of Early American Magazines, 1741-1789.* New York, 1931.

Culture

GENERAL

1 BAILYN, Bernard. "Political Experience and Enlightenment Ideas in Eighteenth-Century America." *Am Hist Rev,* LXVII (1962), 339-351.

2 BARITZ, Loren. *City on a Hill: A History of Ideas and Myths in America.* New York, 1964.†

3 BOORSTIN, Daniel J. *The Americans: The Colonial Experience.* See **22**.5.

4 GARVAN, Anthony. "The New England Plain Style." *Comp Stud Soc Hist,* III (1960), 106-122.

5 KOCH, Adrienne. "Pragmatic Wisdom and the American Enlightenment." *Wm Mar Q,* 3rd ser., XVIII (1961), 313-329.

6 MORISON, Samuel E. *The Intellectual Life of Colonial New England.* 2nd ed. New York, 1956.†

7 SAVELLE, Max. *Seeds of Liberty: The Genesis of the American Mind.* New York, 1948.†

8 TOLLES, Frederick B. "The Culture of Early Pennsylvania." *Pa Mag Hist,* LXXXI (1957), 119-137.

9 TOLLES, Frederick B. *James Logan and the Culture of Provincial America.* Boston, 1957.

10 TOLLES, Frederick B. "'Of the Best Sort but Plain': The Quaker Esthetic." *Am Q,* XI (1959), 484-502.

11 TOLLES, Frederick B. "Quaker Humanist: James Logan as a Classical Scholar." *Pa Mag Hist,* LXXIX (1955), 415-438.

12 WERTENBAKER, Thomas J. *The Founding of American Civilization: The Middle Colonies.* New York, 1938.

13 WERTENBAKER, Thomas J. *The Golden Age of Colonial Culture.* New York, 1942.†

14 WERTENBAKER, Thomas J. *The Old South: The Founding of American Civilization.* New York, 1942.

15 WRIGHT, Louis B. *The Cultural Life of the American Colonies, 1607-1763.* New York, 1957.†

16 WRIGHT, Louis B. "Intellectual History and the Colonial South." *Wm Mar Q,* 3rd ser., XVI (1959), 214-227.

LITERATURE

General

17 GRABO, Norman S. "The Veiled Vision: The Role of Aesthetics in Early American Intellectual History." *Wm Mar Q,* 3rd ser., XIX (1962), 493-510.

18 HUBBELL, Jay B. *The South in American Literature, 1607-1900.* Durham, N.C., 1954.

1 JACKSON, M. Katherine. *Outlines of the Literary History of Colonial Pennsylvania.* Lancaster, Pa., 1906.

2 MURDOCK, Kenneth B. *Literature & Theology in Colonial New England.* Cambridge, Mass., 1949.†

3 PARRINGTON, Vernon L. *Main Currents in American Thought; An Interpretation of American Literature from the Beginning to 1920.* 3 vols., 1927-1930. Vol. I, *The Colonial Mind.* New York, 1927.†

4 PIERCY, Josephine K. *Studies in Literary Types in Seventeenth Century America (1607-1710).* (Yale Studies in English, Vol. XCI). New Haven, 1939.

5 SPILLER, Robert E., and others. *Literary History of the United States.* 3rd ed. 2 vols. New York, 1964.

6 TYLER, Moses C. *A History of American Literature, 1607-1765.* Ithaca, 1949.†

7 WRIGHT, Louis B. "Literature in the Colonial South." *Hunt Lib Q,* X (1947), 297-315.

8 WRIGHT, Luella M. *The Literary Life of the Early Friends, 1650-1725.* New York, 1932.

9 WRIGHT, Thomas G. *Literary Culture in Early New England, 1620-1730.* New Haven, 1920.

Literary Influences: Classical, British, and Continental

10 COOK, Elizabeth C. *Literary Influences in Colonial Newspapers, 1704-1750.* New York, 1912.

11 GUMMERE, Richard M. *The American Colonial Mind and the Classical Tradition: Essays in Comparative Culture.* Cambridge, Mass., 1963.

12 GUMMERE, Richard M. "Apollo on Locust Street." *Pa Mag Hist,* LVI (1932), 68-92.

13 GUMMERE, Richard M. *Seven Wise Men of Colonial America.* Cambridge, Mass., 1967.

14 JACOBSON, D. L. "Thomas Gordon's *Works of Tacitus* in Pre-Revolutionary America." *Bull N Y Pub Lib,* LXIX (1965), 58-64.

15 JONES, Howard M. *America and French Culture, 1750-1848.* Chapel Hill, 1927.

16 LITTO, Frederic M. "Addison's *Cato* in the Colonies." *Wm Mar Q,* 3rd ser., XXIII (1966), 431-449.

17 MYERS, Robert M. "The Old Dominion Looks to London: A Study of English Literary Influence upon *The Virginia Gazette* (1736-1766)." *Va Mag Hist,* LIV (1946), 195-217.

18 SENSABAUGH, George F. *Milton in Early America.* Princeton, 1964.

19 SHIPTON, Clifford K. "Literary Leaven in Provincial New England." *N Eng Q,* IX (1936), 203-217.

20 SIBLEY, Agnes M. *Alexander Pope's Prestige in America, 1725-1835.* New York, 1949.

21 WHEELER, Joseph T. "Literary Culture and Eighteenth Century Maryland: Summary of Findings." *Md Hist Mag,* XXXVIII (1943), 273-276.

22 WILLOUGHBY, Edwin Eliott. "The Reading of Shakespeare in Colonial America." *Pap Bibliog Soc Am,* XXXI (1937), 45-56.

1 WRIGHT, Louis B. "The Classical Tradition in Colonial Virginia." *Pap Bibliog Soc Am,* XXXIII (1939), 85-97.

Poetry

2 CARLISLE, B. F. "The Puritan Structure of Edward Taylor's Poetry." *Am Q,* XX (1968), 147-163.

3 CARLSON, C. Lennart. "Richard Lewis and the Reception of his Work in England." *Am Lit,* IX (1937), 301-316.

4 CARLSON, C. Lennart. "Thomas Godfrey in England." *Am Lit,* VII (1935), 302-309.

5 CROWDER, Richard. *No Featherbed to Heaven: A Biography of Michael Wigglesworth, 1631-1705.* East Lansing, Mich., 1962.

6 FUSSELL, Edwin S. "Benjamin Tompson, Public Poet." *N Eng Q,* XXVI (1953), 494-511.

7 GRABO, Norman S. *Edward Taylor.* New York, 1961.†

8 LEMAY, J. A. Leo. *Ebenezer Kinnersley: Franklin's Friend.* Philadelphia, 1964.

9 LEMAY, J. A. Leo. "Francis Knapp: A Red Herring in Colonial Poetry." *N Eng Q,* XXXIX (1966), 233-237.

10 MATTHIESSEN, F. O. "Michael Wigglesworth, a Puritan Artist." *N Eng Q,* I (1928), 491-504.

11 NORRIS, Walter B. "Some Recently-found Poems on the Calverts." *Md Hist Mag,* XXXII (1943), 112-135.

12 TAYLOR, Edward. *Edward Taylor's Christographia.* New Haven, 1962.

13 TAYLOR, Edward. *The Poems of Edward Taylor.* New Haven, 1960.

14 TAYLOR, Edward. *The Poetical Works of Edward Taylor.* Ed. with intro. by Thomas H. Johnson. Princeton, 1944.

15 THORPE, Peter. "Edward Taylor as Poet." *N Eng Q,* XXXIX (1966), 356-372.

16 WROTH, Lawrence. "James Sterling: Poet, Priest, and Prophet of Empire." *Proc Am Ant Soc,* XLI (1931), 25-76.

Prose

17 BERCOVITCH, Sacvan. "New England Epic: Cotton Mather's *Magnalia Christi Americana.*" *E L H,* XXXIII (1966), 337-350.

18 JONES, Howard M. "American Prose Style: 1700-1770." *Hunt Lib Bull,* No.6 (1934), 115-151.

19 LEMAY, J. A. Leo. "Hamilton's Literary History of the *Maryland Gazette.*" *Wm Mar Q,* 3rd ser., XXIII (1966), 273-285.

20 MIDDLEKAUF, Robert. "Piety and Intellect in Puritanism." *Wm Mar Q,* 3rd ser., XXII (1965), 457-470.

21 SMITH, Peter H. "Politics and Sainthood: Biography by Cotton Mather." *Wm Mar Q,* 3rd ser., XX (1963), 186-206.

22 WROTH, Lawrence C. "The Indian Treaty as Literature." *Yale Rev,* XVII (1928), 749-766.

History

1 COLBOURN, H. Trevor. *The Lamp of Experience: Whig History and the Intellectual Origins of the American Revolution.* Chapel Hill, 1965.

2 GAY, Peter. *A Loss of Mastery. Puritan Historians in Colonial America.* Berkeley, Calif., 1966.

3 PERSONS, Stow. "The Cyclical Theory of History in Eighteenth-Century America." *Am Q,* VI (1954), 147-163.

4 ROBBINS, Caroline. "The 'Excellent Use' of Colonies: A Note on Walter Moyle's Justification of Roman Colonies, ca. 1699." *Wm Mar Q,* 3rd ser., XXIII (1966), 620-621.

Philosophy

5 ALDRIDGE, Alfred O. "Benjamin Franklin and Philosophical Necessity." *Mod Lang Q,* XII (1951), 292-309.

6 ALDRIDGE, Alfred O. "Edwards and Hutcheson." *Har Theol Rev,* XLIV (1951), 35-53.

7 BURANELLI, Vincent. "Colonial Philosophy." *Wm Mar Q,* 3rd ser., XVI (1959), 343-362.

8 COCHRANE, R. C. "Bishop Berkeley and the Progress of the Arts and Learning. Notes on a Literary Convention." *Hunt Lib Q,* XVII (1954), 229-249.

9 DAVIDSON, Edward H. "From Locke to Edwards." *J Hist Ideas,* XXIV (1963), 355-372.

10 LUCE, Arthur A. *The Life of George Berkeley, Bishop of Cloyne.* London, 1949.

11 RAND, Benjamin. *Berkeley's American Sojourn.* Cambridge, Mass., 1932.

12 RILEY, Isaac W. *American Philosophy: The Early Schools* New York, 1958.

SCIENCE

General

13 BELL, Whitfield J. *Early American Science: Needs and Opportunities for Study.* Williamsburg, Va., 1955.

14 BRASCH, Frederick. "The Newtonian Epoch in the American Colonies (1680-1783)." *Proc Am Ant Soc,* new ser., XLIX (1939), 314-332.

15 BRASCH, Frederick. "The Royal Society of London and Its Influence upon Scientific Thought in the American Colonies." *Sci Mo,* XXXIII (1931), 336-355, 448-469.

16 BURSTYN, Harold L. "The Salem Philosophical Library: Its History and Importance for American Science." *Essex Inst Hist Coll,* XCVI (1960), 169-206.

17 COHEN, I. Bernard. *Some Early Tools of American Science: An Account of the Early Scientific Instruments and Biological Collections in Harvard University.* Cambridge, Mass., 1950.

18 DENNY, Margaret. "The Royal Society and American Scholars." *Sci Mo,* LXV (1947), 415-427.

1 FAY, Bernard. "Learned Societies in Europe and America in the Eighteenth Century." *Am Hist Rev,* XXXVII (1932), 255-266.

2 HINDLE, Brooke. *The Pursuit of Science in Revolutionary America, 1735-1789.* Chapel Hill, 1956.†

3 HORNBERGER, Theodore. "Samuel Johnson of Yale and King's College: A Note on the Relation of Science and Religion in Provincial America." *N Eng Q,* VII (1935), 378-397.

4 HORNBERGER, Theodore. *Scientific Thought in the American Colleges, 1638-1800.* Austin, Tex., 1945.

5 JELLISON, Richard M. "Scientific Enquiry in Eighteenth-Century Virginia." *Historian,* XXV (1963), 292-311.

6 KILGOUR, Frederick G. "The Rise of Scientific Activity in Colonial New England." *Yale J Biol Med,* XXII (1949), 123-138.

7 LINGELBACH, William E. "B. Franklin and the Scientific Societies." *Franklin Inst J,* CCLXI (1956), 9-31.

8 MC KEEHAN, Louis W. *Yale Science: The First Hundred Years, 1701-1801.* New York, 1947.

9 STAHLMAN, William D. "Astrology in Colonial America. An Extended Query." *Wm Mar Q,* 3rd ser., XIII (1956), 551-563.

10 STEARNS, Raymond P. "Colonial Fellows of the Royal Society of London, 1661-1788." *Wm Mar Q,* 3rd ser., III (1946), 208-268.

11 STRUIK, Dirk J. *Yankee Science in the Making.* Rev. ed. New York, 1962.

12 WOODFIN, Maude H. "William Byrd and the Royal Society." *Va Mag Hist,* XL (1932), 23-34, 111-123.

Natural History

13 BERKELEY, Edmund and Dorothy S. *John Clayton, Pioneer of American Botany.* Chapel Hill, 1963.

14 BERKELEY, Edmund and Dorothy S., eds. *The Reverend John Clayton, A Parson with a Scientific Mind: His Scientific Writings and Other Related Papers.* Charlottesville, Va., 1965.

15 CLEMENT, John. "Griffith Hughes: S. P. G. Missionary to Pennsylvania and Famous 18th Century Naturalist." *Hist Mag P E Ch,* XVII (1948), 151-163.

16 DENNY, Margaret. "Linnaeus and his Disciple in Carolina: Alexander Garden." *Isis,* XXXVIII (1948), 161-174.

17 EARNEST, Ernest. *John and William Bartram, Botanists and Explorers, 1699-1777, 1739-1823.* Philadelphia, 1940.

18 FRICK, George F. and Raymond P. STEARNS. *Mark Catesby: The Colonial Audubon.* Urbana, Ill., 1961.

19 STANNARD, Jerry. "Early American Botany and its Sources." In *Bibliography and Natural History Essays.* . . . Lawrence, Kan., 1966.

Medicine

20 BEALL, Otho T., Jr. *"Aristotle's Master Piece* in America: A Landmark in the Folklore of Medicine." *Wm Mar Q,* XX (1963), 207-222.

1 BELL, Whitfield J., Jr. "Some American Students of that 'That Shining Oracle of Physic,' Dr. William Cullen of Edinburgh, 1755-1766." *Proc Am Philos Soc,* XCIV (1950), 275-281.

2 BLAKE, John B. "Diseases and Medical Practice in Colonial America." *Int Rec Med,* CLXXI (1958), 350-363.

3 BLAKE, John B. "The Early History of Vital Statistics in Massachusetts." *Bull Hist Med,* XXIX (1955), 46-68.

4 BLAKE, John B. "The Inoculation Controversy in Boston: 1721-1722." *N Eng Q,* XXV (1952), 489-506.

5 BLAKE, John B. *Public Health in the Town of Boston, 1630-1822.* Cambridge, Mass., 1959.

6 BLAKE, John B. "Smallpox Inoculation in Colonial Boston." *J Hist Med,* VIII (1953), 284-300.

7 BLANTON, Wyndham B. *Medicine in Virginia in the Eighteenth Century.* Richmond, Va., 1931.

8 BROWNE, C. A. "Scientific Notes from the Books and Letters of John Winthrop, Jr. (1606-1676) First Governor of Connecticut." *Isis,* XI (1927), 325-342.

9 BROWNE, C. A. "Some Relations of Early Chemistry in America to Medicine." *J Chem Educ,* III (1926), 267-279.

10 CAULFIELD, Ernest. "Infant Feeding in Colonial America." *J Ped,* XLI (1952), 673-687.

11 CAULFIELD, Ernest. "Pediatric Aspects of the Salem Witchcraft Tragedy: A Lesson in Mental Health." *Am J Dis Child,* LXV (1943), 788-802.

12 CAULFIELD, Ernest. "The Pursuit of a Pestilence." *Proc Am Ant Soc,* LX (1950), 21-52.

13 CAULFIELD, Ernest. "Some Common Diseases of Colonial Children." *Pub Col Soc Mass,* XXXV (1951), 4-65.

14 CHILDS, St. Julien R. *Malaria and Colonization in the Carolina Low Country, 1526-1696.* Baltimore, 1940.

15 CHILDS, St. Julien R. "Notes on the History of Public Health in South Carolina, 1670-1800. *Proc S C Hist Assn,* 1932 (1933), 13-22.

16 COWEN, David L. *America's Pre-Pharmacopoeial Literature.* Madison, Wis., 1961.

17 COWEN, David L. *Medicine and Health in New Jersey: A History.* Princeton, 1964.

18 COWEN, David L. "New Jersey Pharmacy and American History." *J Am Phar,* X (1949), 355-360.

19 DRINKER, Cecil K. *Not So Long Ago: A Chronicle of Medicine and Doctors in Colonial Philadelphia.* New York, 1937.

20 DUFFY, John. "Eighteenth-Century Carolina Health Conditions." *J S Hist,* XVIII (1952), 289-302.

21 DUFFY, John. *Epidemics in Colonial America.* See 66.6.

22 DUFFY, John. "Yellow Fever in Colonial Charleston." *S C Hist Mag,* LII (1951), 189-197.

23 FARMER, Laurence. "The Smallpox Inoculation Controversy and the Boston Press, 1721-1722. *Bull N Y Acad Med,* XXXIV (1958), 599-608.

1 FENTON, William N. "Contacts between Iroquois Herbalism and Colonial Medicine." *Ann Rep Smith Inst,* 1941 (1942), 503-526.

2 GUERRA, Francisco. *American Medical Bibliography, 1639-1783.* . . . New York, 1962.

3 GUERRA, Francisco. "Harvey and the Circulation of the Blood in America during the Colonial Period." *Bull Hist Med,* XXXIII (1959), 212-229.

4 HEATON, Claude E. "Medicine in New York during the English Colonial Period, 1664-1775." *Bull Hist Med,* XVII (1945), 9-37.

5 JAMESON, Edwin M. "Eighteenth Century Obstetrics and Obstetricians in the United States." *Ann Med Hist,* X (1938), 413-428.

6 JARCHO, Saul. "Cadwallader Colden as a Student of Infectious Disease." *Bull Hist Med,* XXIX (1955), 99-115.

7 JENKINS, Pierre G. "Alexander Garden, M.D., F.R.S. (1728-1791) Colonial Physician and Naturalist." *Ann Med Hist,* X (1928), 149-158.

8 KRUMBHAAR, E. B. "The State of Pathology in the British Colonies of North America." In *Science, Medicine and History. Essays on the Evolution of Scientific Thought and Medical Practice.* 2 vols. Ed. Ashworth Underwood. London, 1953.

9 *Evolution of Scientific Thought and Medical Practice.* 2 vols. Ed. Ashworth Underwood. London, 1953.

10 MAXWELL, William Q. "A True State of the Smallpox in Williamsburg, February 22, 1748." *Va Mag Hist,* LXIII (1955), 269-274.

11 MILLER, Genevieve. *The Adoption of Inoculation for Smallpox in England and France.* Philadelphia, 1957.

12 MILLER, Genevieve. *Bibliography of the History of Medicine of the United States and Canada, 1939-1960.* Baltimore, 1964. (See also annual bibliographies in *Bulletin of the History of Medicine.*)

13 MILLER, Genevieve. "European Influences in Colonial Medicine." *Ciba,* VIII (1947), 511-521.

14 MILLER, Genevieve. "Smallpox Inoculation in England and America. A Reappraisal." *Wm Mar Q,* 3rd ser., XIII (1956), 476-492.

15 PACKARD, Francis R. *History of Medicine in the United States.* 2 vols. New York, 1963.

16 PACKARD, Francis R. "How London and Edinburgh Influenced Medicine in Philadelphia in the Eighteenth Century." *Ann Med Hist,* IV (1932), 219-244.

17 PACKARD, Francis R. "The Practice of Medicine in Philadelphia in the Eighteenth Century." *Ann Med Hist,* V (1933), 135-150.

18 SHRYOCK, Richard H. "Eighteenth Century Medicine in America." *Proc Am Ant Soc,* LIX (1949), 275-292.

19 SHRYOCK, Richard H. *Medicine and Society in America, 1660-1860.* New York, 1960.†

20 THACHER, James. *American Medical Biography.* . . . Boston, 1828.

21 TWISS, J. R. "Medical Practice in Colonial America." *Bull N Y Acad Med,* XXXVI (1960), 538-551.

22 VIETS, Henry R. "Some Features of the History of Medicine in Massachusetts during the Colonial Period (1620-1770)." *Isis,* XXIII (1935), 389-405.

23 WARING, Joseph I. *A History of Medicine in South Carolina, 1670-1825.* Columbia, S.C., 1964.

1 WARING, Joseph I. "St. Philip's Hospital in Charlestown in Carolina; Medical Care of the Poor in Colonial Times." *Ann Med Hist,* IV (1932), 283-289.

2 WEAVER, J. Calvin. "Early Medical History of Georgia: Georgia as a Colony." *J Med Assn Ga,* XXIX (1940), 89-112.

Chemistry

3 COHEN, I. Bernard. "The Beginning of Chemical Instruction in America: A Brief Account of the Teaching of Chemistry at Harvard Prior to 1800." *Chymia,* III (1950), 17-44.

Physics and Astronomy

4 ALDRIDGE, Alfred O. "Benjamin Franklin and Jonathan Edwards on Lightning and Earthquakes." *Isis,* XLI (1950), 162-164.

5 CLARK, Charles E. "Science, Reason, and an Angry God: The Literature of an Earthquake." *N Eng Q,* XXXVIII (1965), 340-362.

6 COHEN, I Bernard. *Franklin and Newton. An Inquiry into Speculative Newtonian Experimental Science and Franklin's Work in Electricity as an Example Thereof.* Philadelphia, 1956.

7 HINDLE, Brooke. "Cadwallader Colden's Extension of the Newtonian Principles." *Wm Mar Q,* XIII (1956), 459-475.

8 MC KILLOP, Alan D. "Some Newtonian Verses in 'Poor Richard.'" *N Eng Q,* XXI (1948), 383-385.

9 MENDELSOHN, Everett. "John Lining and his Contribution to Early American Science. *Isis,* LI (1960), 278-292.

10 MORSE, William N. "Lectures on Electricity in Colonial Times." *N Eng Q,* VII (1934), 364-374.

11 STEEDMAN, Marguerite. "John Lining. Southern Scientist." *Ga Rev,* X (1956), 334-345.

12 TILTON, Eleanor M. "Lightning-Rods and the Earthquake of 1755." *N Eng Q,* XIII (1940), 85-97.

13 TOLLES, Frederick B. "Philadelphia's First Scientist, James Logan." *Isis,* XLVII (1956), 20-30.

14 WOOLF, Harry. *The Transit of Venus: A Study of Eighteenth-Century Science.* Princeton, 1959.

Mapmaking

15 GIPSON, Lawrence H. *Lewis Evans, ...* Philadelphia, 1939.

Technology

16 HINDLE, Brooke. *Technology in Early America. Needs and Opportunities for Study. . . .* Chapel Hill, 1966.

17 OLIVER, John W. *History of American Technology (1607-1955).* New York, 1956.

THE FINE ARTS
General

1 *Boston Museum of Fine Arts, Eighteenth-Century American Arts: The M. and M. Karolik Collection of Paintings, Drawings, Engravings, Furniture, Silver, Needlework and Incidental Objects.* Cambridge, Mass., 1941.

2 GOWANS, Alan. *Images of American Living.* Philadelphia, 1964.

3 GROCE, George C. and David H. WALLACE. *The New York Historical Society's Dictionary of Artists in America, 1564-1860.* New Haven, 1957.

4 LARKIN, Oliver W. *Art and Life in America.* New York, 1949.

5 LIPMAN, Jean H. *American Folk Art in Wood, Metal and Stone.* New York, 1948.

6 WHITEHILL, Walter Muir. *The Arts in Early American History: Needs and Opportunities for Study, An Essay.* Chapel Hill, 1965.

7 WRIGHT, Louis B., George B. TATUM, John C. MC COUBREY, and Robert C. SMITH. *The Arts in America: The Colonial Period.* New York, 1966.

Architecture

General

8 ANDREWS, Wayne. *Architecture, Ambition and Americans.* New York, 1955.†

9 EBERLEIN, Harold D. and Cortlandt HUBBARD. *American Georgian Architecture.* Bloomington, Ind., 1952.

10 HOWELLS, John M. *Lost Examples of Colonial Architecture.* New York, 1931.

11 JACKSON, Joseph. *American Colonial Architecture, its Origin and Development.* Philadelphia, 1924.

12 KIMBALL, Fiske. "Architecture in the History of the Colonies and of the Republic." *Am Hist Rev,* XXVII (1921), 47-57.

13 MORRISON, Hugh S. *Early American Architecture, from the first Colonial Settlements to the National Period.* New York, 1952.

14 MUMFORD, Lewis. *Sticks and Stones: A Study of American Architecture and Civilization.* 2nd ed., rev. New York, 1955.†

15 PARKS, Helen. "A List of Architectural Books Available in America before the Revolution." *J Soc Arch Hist.* XX (1961), 115-130.

16 ROOS, Frank J. *Writings on Early American Architecture: An Annotated List . . .* Columbus, Ohio, 1943.

Civic Architecture and Town Planning

17 CADY, John Hutchings. *The Civic and Architectural Development of Providence, 1636-1950.* Providence, 1957.

18 COUSINS, Frank and Philip M. RILEY. *The Colonial Architecture of Philadelphia.* Boston, 1920.

1 COUSINS, Frank and Philip M. RILEY. *Colonial Architecture of Salem.* Boston, 1919.

2 DOWNING, Antoinette F. and Vincent J. SCULLY Jr. *The Architectural Heritage of Newport, Rhode Island, 1640-1915.* Cambridge, Mass., 1952.

3 EBERLEIN, Harold D. and Cortlandt HUBBARD. *Portrait of a Colonial City: Philadelphia, 1670-1838.* Philadelphia, 1939.

4 GARVAN, Anthony N. B. *Architecture and Town Planning in Colonial Connecticut.* New Haven, 1951.

5 KOCHER, A. Lawrence and Howard DEARSTYNE. *Colonial Williamsburg, Its Buildings and Gardens. . . .* Rev. ed. New York, 1961.

6 KOUWENHOVEN, John A. *The Columbia Historical Portrait of New York: An Essay in Graphic History in Honor of the Tricentennial of New York City and the Bicentennial of Columbia University.* Garden City, N. Y., 1953.

7 MURTAGH, William J. *Moravian Architecture and Town Planning.* Ann Arbor, Mich., 1963.

8 REPS, John W. *The Making of Urban America; A History of City Planning in the United States.* Princeton, 1965.

9 STOKES, I. N. Phelps. *The Iconography of Manhattan Island, 1498-1909.* 6 vols. New York, 1915-1928.

10 WHIFFEN, Marcus. *The Eighteenth-Century Houses of Williamsburg: A Study of Architecture and Building in the Colonial Capital of Virginia.* New York, 1960.

11 WHIFFEN, Marcus. *The Public Buildings of Williamsburg.* New York, 1958.

12 WHITEHILL, Walter Muir. *Boston, A Topographical History.* Cambridge, Mass., 1959.

Church Architecture

13 BROCK, Henry Irving. *Colonial Churches in Virginia.* Richmond, Va., 1930.

14 DORSEY, Stephen D. *Early English Churches in America, 1607-1807.* New York 1952.

15 KELLY, J. Frederick. *Early Connecticut Meetinghouses . . . Before 1830 Based Chiefly upon Town and Parish Records.* 2 vols. New York, 1948.

16 MASON, George C. *Colonial Churches of Tidewater Virginia.* Richmond, Va., 1945.

17 METCALF, Priscilla. "Boston before Bulfinch: Harrison's Kings' Chapel." *J Soc Arch Hist,* XIII (1954), 11-14.

18 RINES, Edward F. *Old Historic Churches of America.* New York, 1936.

19 ROSE, Harold W. *The Colonial Houses of Worship in America. . . .* New York, 1963.

20 WALLACE, Philip B. and William A. DUNN. *Colonial Churches and Meeting Houses; Pennsylvania, New Jersey and Delaware.* New York, 1931.

Domestic Architecture

21 BAILEY, Rosalie F. *Pre-Revolutionary Dutch Houses and Families in Northern New Jersey and Southern New York.* New York, 1936.

1 BRIGGS, Martin S. *The Homes of the Pilgrim Fathers in England and America*. New York, 1932.

2 BRUMBAUGH, G. Edwin. *Colonial Architecture of the Pennsylvania Germans*. Lancaster, Pa., 1933.

3 COFFIN, Lewis and Arthur C. HOLDEN. *Brick Architecture of the Colonial Period in Maryland and Virginia*. New York, 1919.

4 DAVIS, Deering. *Annapolis Houses, 1700-1775*. New York, 1947.

5 DE LAGERBERG, Lars. *New Jersey Architecture; Colonial and Federal*. Springfield, Mass., 1956.

6 DOWNING, Antoinette F. *Early Homes of Rhode Island*. Richmond, Va., 1937.

7 EBERLEIN, Harold D. *Historic Houses and Buildings of Delaware*. Dover, Del., 1962.

8 EBERLEIN, Harold D. *Historic Houses of the Hudson Valley*. New York, 1942.

9 FORMAN, Henry C. *The Architecture of the Old South: The Medieval Style, 1585-1850*. Cambridge, Mass., 1948.

10 FORMAN, Henry C. *Early Manor and Plantation Houses of Maryland. 1634-1800*. Easton, Pa., 1934.

11 FORMAN, Henry C. *Tidewater Maryland Architecture and Gardens*. New York, 1956.

12 GOWANS, Alan. *Architecture in New Jersey: A Record of American Civilization*. Princeton, 1964.

13 JOHNSTON, Frances Benjamin, and Thomas Tileston WATERMAN. *The Early Architecture of North Carolina. A Pictorial Survey with an Architectural History*. Chapel Hill, 1941.

14 KELLY, John Frederick. *Early Domestic Architecture of Connecticut*. New Haven, 1924.

15 KIMBALL, Fiske. *Domestic Architecture of the American Colonies and of the Early Republic*. New York, 1922.

16 LEIDING, Harriette K. *Historic Houses of South Carolina*. Philadelphia, 1921.

17 NICHOLS, Frederick Doveton. *The Early Architecture of Georgia*. Chapel Hill, 1957.

18 REYNOLDS, Helen W. *Dutch Houses in the Hudson Valley before 1776*. New York, 1929.

19 SALE, Edith T. *Interiors of Virginia Houses of Colonial Times, from the Beginnings of Virginia to the Revolution*. Richmond, Va., 1927.

20 SALE, Edith T. *Manors of Virginia in Colonial Times*. Philadelphia, 1909.

21 SHURTLEFF, Harold R. *The Log Cabin Myth; A Study of the Early Dwelling of the English Colonists in North America*. Cambridge, Mass., 1939.

22 STONEY, Samuel G. *Plantations of the Carolina Low Country*. Charleston, S.C., 1938.

1 THWING, Leroy L. "Lighting in Early Colonial Massachusetts." *N Eng Q,* XI (1938), 166-170.

2 WAINWRIGHT, Nicholas B. *Colonial Grandeur in Philadelphia: The House and Furniture of General John Cadwalader.* Philadelphia, 1964.

3 WALLACE, Philip B. *Colonial Houses, Philadelphia, Pre-Revolutionary Period.* New York, 1931.

4 WATERMAN, Thomas T. *The Dwellings of Colonial America.* Chapel Hill, 1950.

5 WATERMAN, Thomas T. *The Mansions of Virginia, 1706-1776.* Chapel Hill, 1946.

6 WATERMAN, Thomas T. and John A. BARROWS. *Domestic Colonial Architecture of Tidewater Virginia.* New York, 1932.

7 WORTH, Henry B. *The Development of the New England Dwelling House.* Lynn, Mass., 1911.

Farm Buildings

8 DORNBUSCH, Charles H. *Pennsylvania German Barns.* Allentown, Pa., 1958.

9 SHOEMAKER, Alfred L., ed. *The Pennsylvania Barn.* Kutztown, Pa., 1959.

Architects

10 BEIRNE, Rosamond R. and John H. SCARFF. *William Buckland, Architect of Virginia and Maryland.* Baltimore, 1958.

11 BRIDENBAUGH, Carl. *Peter Harrison: First American Architect.* Chapel Hill, 1949.

12 RAVENEL, Beatrice. *Architects of Charleston.* Charleston, 1945.

Painting

13 BARKER, Vergil. *American Painting, History, and Interpretation.* New York, 1950.

14 BELKNAP, Waldron Phoenix, Jr. *American Colonial Painting: Materials for a History.* Ed. Charles Coleman Sellers. Cambridge, Mass., 1959.

15 BURROUGHS, Alan. *John Greenwood in America, 1745-1752: A Monograph with Notes and a Check List.* Andover, 1943.

16 FLEXNER, John T. *American Painting.* 2 vols. Boston, 1947.

17 FLOURNOY, Mary H. "Art in the Early South." *S Atl Q,* XXIX (1930), 402-418.

18 FOOTE, Henry W. "Charles Bridges: "Sergeant-Painter of Virginia." *Va Mag Hist,* LX (1952), 3-55.

19 FOOTE, Henry W. *Robert Feke, Colonial Portrait Painter.* Cambridge, Mass., 1930.

20 HENSEL, William. "Jacob Eichholz, Painter." *Pa Mag Hist,* XXXVII (1913), 48-75.

21 HOWLAND, Garth A. "John Valentine Haidt, A Little Known Eighteenth Century Painter." *Pa Mag Hist,* VIII (1941), 304-313.

1 LIPMAN, Jean H. and Alice WINCHESTER. *Primitive Painters in America; 1750-1950: An Anthology.* New York, 1950.

2 LYMAN, Lila P. "William Johnston (1732-1772): A Forgotten Portrait Painter of New England." *N Y Hist Soc Q,* XXXIX (1955), 62-78.

3 MC COUBREY, John W. *American Tradition in Painting.* New York, 1963.

4 MIDDLETON, Margaret S. *Jeremiah Theus, Colonial Artist of Charles Town.* New York, 1953.

5 PARK, Lawrence. *Joseph Blackburn, A Colonial Portrait Painter; with a Descriptive List of his Works.* Worcester, Mass., 1923.

6 PLEASANTS, Jacob H. "Justus Engelhardt Kuhn (d. 1717) an Early Eighteenth Century Maryland Portrait Painter." *Proc Am Ant Soc,* XLVI (1937), 243-280.

7 PLEASANTS, Jacob H. "William Dering: A Mid-Eighteenth Century Williamsburg Portrait Painter." *Va Mag Hist,* LX (1952), 56-63.

8 RICHARDSON, E. P. "Gustavus Hesselius." *Art Q,* XII (1949), 220-226.

9 RICHARDSON, Edgar P. *Painting in America: The Story of 450 Years.* New York, 1956.

10 SELLERS, Charles Coleman. *Benjamin Franklin in Portraiture.* New Haven, 1962.

11 WHEELER, Robert G. "The Use of Symbolism in Hudson Valley Painting of the Early 18th Century." *N Y Hist,* XXXVI (1955), 357-362.

Stonecarving and Woodcarving

12 BREWINGTON, M. V. *Shipcarvers of North America.* Barre, Mass., 1962.

13 FORBES, H. M. *Gravestones of Early New England and the Men who made them, 1653-1800.* Boston, 1927.

14 LUDWIG, Allen I. *Graven Images: New England Stonecarving and its Symbols, 1650-1815.* Middletown, Conn., 1966.

Metalwork

15 AVERY, Clara Louise. *Early American Silver.* New York, 1930.

16 Boston Museum of Fine Arts. *Colonial Silversmiths, Masters and Apprentices.* Boston, 1956.

17 BUHLER, Katheryn C. *American Silver.* Cleveland, Ohio, 1950.

18 FALES, Martha G. *American Silver in the Henry Francis du Pont Winterthur Museum.* Winterthur, Del., 1958.

19 KAUFFMAN, Henry. *Early American Copper, Tin and Brass.* New York, 1950.

20 LAUGHLIN, Ledlie I. *Pewter in America, Its Makers and Their Marks.* Boston, 1940.

1 PHILLIPS, John M. *American Silver.* New York, 1949.

2 SONN, Albert H. *Early American Wrought Iron.* New York, 1928.

3 WALLACE, Philip B. *Colonial Ironwork in Old Philadelphia.* New York, 1930.

Ceramics

4 CLEMENT, Arthur W. *Our Pioneer Potters.* New York, 1947.

5 WATKINS, Laura W. *Early New England Potters and Their Wares.* Cambridge, Mass., 1950.

Textiles

6 LITTLE, Frances. *Early American Textiles.* New York, 1931.

Furniture

7 BJERKIE, Ethel H. *The Cabinetmakers of America.* Garden City, N.Y., 1957.

8 COMSTOCK, Helen. *American Furniture: A Complete Guide to Seventeenth, Eighteenth, and Nineteenth Century Styles.* New York, 1962.

9 DOWNS, Joseph. *American Furniture: Queen Anne and Chippendale Periods in the Henry Francis du Pont Winterthur Museum.* New York, 1952.

10 HIPKISS, Edwin J. *Eighteenth Century American Arts.* Cambridge, Mass., 1941.

11 KETTELL, Russell H. *The Pine Furniture of Early New England.* New York, 1929.

12 LOCKWOOD, Luke V. *Colonial Furniture in America.* 2 vols. New York, 1926.

13 NAGEL, Charles. *American Furniture, 1650-1850: A Brief Background and an Illustrated History.* New York, 1949.

14 ORMSBEE, Thomas H. *Early American Furniture Markers, A Social and Biographical Study.* New York, 1957.

Landscape Gardening

15 HART, Bertha S. "The First Garden of Georgia." *Ga Hist Q,* XIX (1935), 325-332.

16 MATHER, Edith H. "John Reid of Hortensia: First Landscape Architect to Come to America." *Proc N J Hist Soc,* LV (1937), 1-20.

17 STETSON, Sarah P. "American Garden Books, Transplanted and Native, before 1807." *Wm Mar Q,* 3rd ser., III (1946), 343-369.

MUSIC

18 CHANCELLOR, Paul G. "Pennsylvania's Colonial Influences on American Musical History." *Etude,* LXVI (1948), 75, 122-123, 147, 186, 221, 256, 266.

19 COVEY, Cyclone. "Puritanism and Music in Colonial America." *Wm Mar Q,* 3rd ser., VIII (1951), 378-388.

20 FOOTE, Henry W. "Musical Life in Boston in the Eighteenth Century." *Proc Am Ant Soc,* XLIX (1940), 293-313.

1 MC CORKLE, Donald M. "The Moravian Contribution to American Music (1740-1840)." *Notes,* XIII (1956), 597-603.

2 MAC DOUGALL, Hamilton C. *Early New England Psalmody: An Historical Appreciation, 1620-1820.* Brattleboro, Vt., 1940.

3 MAURER, Maurer. "The 'Professor of Musick' in Colonial America." *Mus Q,* XXXVI (1950), 511-524.

4 SCHOLES, Percy A. *The Puritans and Music in England and New England: A Contribution to the Cultural History of Two Nations.* London, 1934.

5 SCHOLES, Percy A. "The Truth about the New England Puritans and Music." *Mus Q,* XIX (1933), 1-17.

6 SONNECK, Oscar G. T. *Early Concert-Life in America.* New York, 1949.

POPULAR CULTURE

General

7 CARSON, Jane. *Colonial Virginians at Play.* Williamsburg, Va., 1965.

8 CLARK, William B. "The Sea Captains Club." *Pa Mag Hist,* LXXXI (1957), 39-68.

9 DULLES, Foster R. *America Learns to Play; A History of Popular Recreation, 1607-1940.* New York, 1940.†

10 TATSCH, J. Hugo. *Freemasonry in the Thirteen Colonies.* New York, 1929.

Theatre

11 BROWN, Benjamin W. *The Colonial Theatre in New England.* Newport, R.I., 1930.

12 COLE, Arthur C. "The Puritan and Fair Terpischore." *Miss Val Hist Rev,* XXIX (1942), 3-34.

13 LAND, Robert H. "The First Williamsburg Theater." *Wm Mar Q,* 3rd ser., V (1948), 359-374.

14 LAW, Robert A. "A Diversion for Colonial Gentlemen." *Tex Rev,* II (1916), 79-88.

15 POLLOCK, Thomas C. *The Philadelphia Theatre in the Eighteenth Century, Together with the Daybook of the Same Period.* Philadelphia, 1933.

16 RANKIN, Hugh F. *The Theater in Colonial America.* Chapel Hill, 1965.

17 WILLIS, Eola. *The Charleston Stage in the Eighteenth Century.* Columbia, S.C., 1924.

Religion

GENERAL

18 BRIDENBAUGH, Carl. *Mitre and Sceptre: Transatlantic Faiths, Ideas, Personalities, and Politics, 1689-1775.* New York, 1962.†

19 HEIMERT, Alan. *Religion and the American Mind from the Great Awakening to the Revolution.* Cambridge, Mass., 1966.

1 MEAD, Sidney E. "Denominationalism: The Shape of Protestantism in America." *Ch Hist,* XXII (1953), 279-297; XXIII (1954), 291-320.

2 MEAD, Sidney E. "From Coercion to Persuasion. Another Look at the Rise of Religious Liberty and the Emergence of Denominationalism (1607-1791)." *Ch Hist,* XXV (1956), 317-337.

3 MEAD, Sidney E. *The Lively Experiment: The Shaping of Christianity in America.* New York, 1963.

4 MILLER, Perry. *Nature's Nation.* Cambridge, Mass., 1967.

5 NEWLIN, Claude M. *Philosophy and Religion in Colonial America.* New York, 1962.

6 NIEBUHR, H. Richard. *The Kingdom of God in America.* New York, 1959.†

7 NIEBUHR, H. Richard. *The Social Sources of Denominationalism.* New York, 1957.†

8 SMITH, James W. and A. Leland JAMISON. *Religion in American Life.* 2 vols. Princeton, 1961

9 SMITH, Timothy L. "Congregation, State, and Denomination: The Framing of the American Religious Structure." *Wm Mar Q,* 3rd ser., XXV (1968), 155-176.

10 SWEET, William W. *Religion in Colonial America.* New York, 1942.

11 WEIS, Frederick L. *The Colonial Churches and the Colonial Clergy of the Middle and Southern Colonies, 1607-1776.* Lancaster, Mass., 1938.

12 WEIS, Frederick L. *The Colonial Clergy and the Colonial Churches of New England.* Lancaster, Mass., 1936.

13 WEIS, Frederick L. *The Colonial Clergy of Maryland, Delaware, and Georgia.* Lancaster, Mass., 1950.

14 WEIS, Frederick L. *The Colonial Clergy of Virginia, North Carolina, and South Carolina.* Boston, 1955.

THE ANGLICAN CHURCH

15 BRYDON, George M. *Virginia's Mother Church and the Political Conditions under which it Grew: An Interpretation of the Records of the Colony of Virginia and of the Anglican Church of that Colony. 1607-1727.* Richmond, Va., 1947.

16 BRYDON, GEORGE M. *Virginia's Mother Church and the Political Conditions under which it Grew: The Story of the Anglican Church and the Development of Religion in Virginia, 1727-1814.* Philadelphia, 1952.

17 BURR, Nelson R. *The Anglican Church in New Jersey.* Philadelphia, 1954.

18 CHORLEY, E. Clowes. "The Beginnings of the Church in the Province of New York." *Hist Mag P E Ch,* XIII (1944), 5-25.

19 CLEMENT, John. "Anglican Clergymen Licensed to the American Colonies, 1710-1744." *Hist Mag P E Ch,* XVII (1948), 207-250.

20 CURTIS, L. P. *Anglican Moods of the Eighteenth Century.* Hamden, Conn., 1966.

21 DAVIDSON, Elizabeth. *The Establishment of the English Church in Continental American Colonies.* Durham, N.C., 1936.

1 EDWARDS, Maldwyn. *John Wesley and the Eighteenth Century: A Study of His Social and Political Influence.* Cincinnati, 1933.

2 ERVIN, Spencer. "The Anglican Church in North Carolina, 1663-1823." *Hist Mag P E Ch,* XXV (1956), 102-161.

3 ERVIN, Spencer. "The Established Church of Colonial Maryland." *Hist Mag P E Ch,* XXIV (1955), 232-292.

4 ERVIN, Spencer. "The Establishment, Government, and Functioning of the Church in Colonial Virginia." *Hist Mag P E Ch,* XXVI (1957), 65-110.

5 GREENE, Evarts B. "The Anglican Outlook on the American Colonies in the Early Eighteenth Century." *Am Hist Rev,* XX (1914), 64-85.

6 JOHNSTON, Gideon. *Carolina Chronicle: The Papers of Commissary Gideon Johnston, 1707-1716.* Ed Frank J. Klingberg. Berkeley, Calif., 1946.

7 KEEN, Quentin B. "The Problems of a Commissary: The Reverend Alexander Garden of South Carolina." *Hist Mag P E Ch,* XX (1951), 136-155.

8 KIRBY, Ethyn (Williams). *George Keith, 1638-1716.* New York, 1942.

9 KLINGBERG, Frank J. "The Expansion of the Anglican Church in the Eighteenth Century." *Hist Mag P E Ch,* XVI (1947), 292-301.

10 LAMB, George W. "Clergymen Licensed to the American Colonies by the Bishops of London, 1745-1781. *Hist Mag P E Ch,* XIII (1944), 128-143.

11 LE JAU, Francis. *The Carolina Chronicle of Dr. Francis Le Jau, 1706-1717.* Ed. Frank J. Klingberg. Berkeley, Calif., 1956.

12 LYDEKKER, John W. "Thomas Bray (1658-1730), Founder of Missionary Enterprise." *Hist Mag P E Ch,* XII (1943), 187-214.

13 PENNINGTON, Edgar L. "The Beginning of the Church of England in South Carolina." *Hist Mag P E Ch,* II (1933), 178-194.

14 PENNINGTON, Edgar L. "Beginnings of the Church of England in Georgia." *Hist Mag P E Ch,* I (1932), 222-234.

15 PENNINGTON, Edgar L *Commissary Blair.* Hartford, Conn., 1936.

16 PENNINGTON, Edgar L. "John Wesley's Georgia Ministry." *Ch Hist,* VIII (1939), 231-254.

17 PENNINGTON, Edgar L. "The Reverend Alexander Garden." *Hist Mag P E Ch,* III (1934), 48-55, 111-119.

18 RIGHTMYER, Nelson W. *The Anglican Church in Delaware.* Philadelphia, 1947.

19 RIGHTMYER, Nelson W. "The Character of the Anglican Clergy of Colonial Maryland." *Md Hist Mag,* XLIV (1949), 229-250.

20 RIGHTMYER, Nelson W. *Maryland's Established Church.* Baltimore, 1956.

21 SEILER, William H. "The Anglican Parish Vestry in Colonial Virginia." *J S Hist,* XXII (1956), 310-337.

22 SEILER, William H. "The Church of England as the Established Church in Seventeenth-Century Virginia." *J S Hist,* XV (1949), 478-508.

1 ZABRISKIE, Alexander C. "The Rise and Main Characteristics of the Anglican Evangelical Movement in England and America." *Hist Mag P E Ch*, XII (1943), 83-115.

PURITANISM AND CONGREGATIONALISM

2 GOODWIN, Gerald J. "The Myth of 'Arminian Calvinism.'" *N Eng Q*, XLI (1968), 213-237.

3 LOCKRIDGE, Kenneth A. "The History of a Puritan Church, 1637-1736." *N Eng Q*, XL (1967), 399-424.

4 MILLER, Perry. *Errand into the Wilderness*. Cambridge, Mass., 1956.† .

5 MILLER, Perry. *The New England Mind: From Colony to Province*. See 76.10.

6 MILLER, Perry and Thomas H. JOHNSON, eds. *The Puritans*. New York, 1938.†

7 OBERHOLZER, Emil, Jr. *Delinquent Saints. Disciplinary Action in the Early Congregational Churches of Massachusetts*. New York, 1956.

8 TREFZ, Edward K. "Satan as the Prince of Evil: The Preaching of New England Puritans." *Bos Pub Lib Q*, VII (1955), 3-22.

9 TREFZ, Edward K. "Satan in Puritan Preaching (1644-1747)." *Bos Pub Lib Q*, VIII (1956), 71-84, 148-159.

10 WHITTEMORE, Robert C. "The Coherent Calvinism of Samuel Willard." *Ch Hist*, XXXVI (1967), 284-298.

11 WINSLOW, Ola E. *Meetinghouse Hill, 1630-1783*. New York, 1952.

Jonathan Edwards

12 CARSE, James. *Jonathan Edwards and the Visibility of God*. New York, 1967.

13 ELWOOD, Douglas J. *The Philosophical Theology of Jonathan Edwards*. New York, 1960.

14 GOEN, C. C. "Jonathan Edwards: A New Departure in Eschatology." *Ch Hist*, XXVIII (1959), 25-40.

15 HAROUTUNIAN, Joseph G. "Jonathan Edwards, Theologian of the Great Commandment." *Theo Today*, I (1944), 361-377.

16 MILLER, Perry. *Jonathan Edwards*. See 25.1.

17 PARKER, Gail Thain. "Jonathan Edwards and Melancholy." *N Eng Q*, XLI (1968), 193-212.

18 PIERCE, David C. "Jonathan Edwards and the 'New Sense of Glory,'" *N Eng Q*, XLI (1968), 82-95.

19 RHOADES, Donald H. "Jonathan Edwards: America's First Philosopher." *Person*, XXXIII (1952), 135-147.

20 SUTER, Rufus. "The Concept of Morality in the Philosophy of Jonathan Edwards." *J Rel*, XIV (1934), 265-272.

21 THOMAS, Vincent. "The Modernity of Jonathan Edwards." *N Eng Q*, XXV (1952), 60-84.

THE REFORMED DUTCH CHURCH

1 CORWIN, Charles E. *A Manual of the Reformed Church in America (Formerly Reformed Protestant Dutch Church) 1628-1922.* 5th ed. New York, 1922.

2 CORWIN, Samuel T. *History of the Dutch Reformed Church in the United States.* New York, 1895.

THE FRENCH HUGUENOT REFORMED CHURCH

3 BAIRD, George W. *History of the Huguenot Emigration to America.* See **44**.11.

4 BULTMANN, William A. "The S.P.G. and the French Huguenots in Colonial America." *Hist Mag P E Ch,* XX (1951), 156-172.

5 DOUGLAS, Donald. *The Huguenot.* See **44**.13.

6 DUCLOS, R. P. *Histoire du Protestantisme Français.* See **44**.14.

7 HIRSCH, Arthur H. *The Huguenots of Colonial South Carolina.* See **44**.15.

SOCIETY OF FRIENDS

8 BRAITHWAITE, William C. *The Beginnings of Quakerism.* Rev. and annotated by Henry J. Cadbury. New York, 1955.

9 BRAITHWAITE, William C. *The Second Period of Quakerism.* Rev. and annotated by Henry J. Cadbury. New York, 1961.

10 CADY, Edwin H. *John Woolman: The Mind of the Quaker Saint.* New York, 1966.

11 JAMES, Sydney V. *A People among Peoples: Quaker Benevolence in Eighteenth-Century America.* Cambridge, Mass., 1963.

12 JONES, Rufus M. *The Quakers in the American Colonies.* London, 1911.†

13 THOMAS, Allen C. *A History of the Friends in America.* Philadelphia, 1930.

14 TOLLES, Frederick B. *The Atlantic Community of the Early Friends.* London, 1952.

15 WHITNEY, Jane P. *John Woolman, American Quaker.* Boston, 1942.

PRESBYTERIANS

16 DRURY, Clifford M. "Presbyterian Beginnings in New England and the Middle Colonies (1640-1714). *J Presby Hist Soc,* XXXIV (1956), 19-35.

17 FUNK, Henry D. "The Influence of the Presbyterian Church in Early American History." *J Presby Hist Soc,* XII (1924), 26-63; XIII (1925), 152-189; XIV (1926), 281-316.

1 KLETT, Guy S. *Presbyterians in Colonial Pennsylvania.* Philadelphia, 1937.

2 SCOTT, Robert F. "Colonial Presbyterianism in the Valley of Virginia, 1727-1775." *J Presby Hist Soc,* XXXV (1957), 71-92, 171-192.

3 THOMPSON, Ernest T. *Presbyterians in the South.* Vol. I, 1607-1861. Richmond, Va., 1963.

4 TRINTERUD, Leonard J. *The Forming of an American Tradition: A Re-Examination of Colonial Presbyterianism.* Philadelphia, 1949.

GERMAN RELIGIOUS GROUPS

Lutheranism

5 QUALBEN, Lars P. *The Lutheran Church in Colonial America.* New York, 1940.

6 SCHMAUK, Theodore E. *A History of the Lutheran Church in Pennsylvania (1638-1820). . . .* Philadelphia, 1903.

German Reformed

7 HINKE, William J. *Life and Letters of the Rev. John Philip Boehm, Founder of the Reformed Church in Pennsylvania, 1683-1749.* Philadelphia, 1916.

Pietism

General

8 BITTINGER, Lucy F. *German Religious Life in Colonial Times.* Philadelphia, 1907.

9 BROWN, J. A. "The Pietistic Controversy." *Q Rev Evan Luth Ch,* IV (1874), 278-301.

10 HOSKINS, John P. "German Influence on Religious Life and Thought in America during the Colonial Period." *Princ Theo Rev,* V (1907), 49-79, 210-241.

11 SACHSE, Julius F. *German Pietists of Provincial Pennsylvania, 1694-1708.* Philadelphia, 1895.

12 STOEFFLER, E. Ernest. *Mysticism in the German Devotional Literature of Colonial Pennsylvania.* Allentown, Pa., 1950.

13 WOOD, Ralph, ed. *The Pennsylvania Germans.* See **46.14.**

14 WUST, Klaus G. "German Mystics and Sabbatarians in Virginia, 1700-1764." *Va Mag Hist,* LXXII (1964), 330-347.

Moravians

15 HAMILTON, John T. *A History of the Church Known as the Moravian Church.* Bethlehem, Pa., 1900.

16 KOHNOVA, Marie J. "The Moravians and their Missionaries, a Problem in Americanization." *Miss Val Hist Rev,* XIX (1932), 348-361.

17 SESSLER, Jacob J. *Communal Pietism among Early American Moravians.* New York, 1933.

18 WEINLICK, John R. "Colonial Moravians, Their Status among the Churches." *Pa Hist,* XXVI (1959), 213-225.

1 WEINLICK, John R. *Count Zinzendorf.* Nashville, Tenn., 1956.

German Baptists

2 AURAND, A. Monroe, Jr. *Historical Account of the Ephrata Cloister and the Seventh Day Baptist Society.* Harrisburg, Pa., 1940.

3 SACHSE, Julius F. *The German Sectarians of Pennsylvania, 1708-1742, A Critical and Legendary History of the Ephrata Cloister and the Dunkers.* 2 vols. Philadelphia, 1899-1901.

Mennonites

4 SMITH, C. Henry. "The Mennonite Immigration to Pennsylvania in the Eighteenth Century." *Proc Pa-Ger Soc,* XXV (1925), 1-142.

5 SOUDER, John D. "The Life and Times of Dielman Kolb." *Menn Q Rev,* II (1929), 33-41.

Church of the Brethren

6 DURNBAUGH, Donald F. *European Origins of the Brethren: A Source Book on the Beginnings of the Church of the Brethren in the Early Eighteenth Century.* Elgin, Ill., 1958.

ROMAN CATHOLICISM

7 ELLIS, John T. *Catholics in Colonial America.* Baltimore, 1965.

8 KENNEDY, William H. J. "Catholics in Massachusetts before 1750." *Cath Hist Rev,* XVII (1931), 10-28.

9 MARRARO, Howard R. "Rome and the Catholic Church in Eighteenth-Century American Magazines." *Cath Hist Rev,* XXXII (1946), 157-189.

10 NUESSE, Celestine J. *The Social Thought of American Catholics, 1634-1829.* Westminster, Md., 1945.

11 PHELAN, Thomas P. *Catholics in Colonial Days.* New York, 1935.

12 RAY, Sister Mary Augustina. *American Opinion of Roman Catholicism in The Eighteenth Century.* New York, 1936.

13 RILEY, Arthur J. *Catholicism in New England to 1788.* Washington, D.C., 1936.

JUDAISM

For further references see the section on Jews under Economic and Social Development: Immigration.

14 MARCUS, Jacob R. *Early American Jewry.* 2 vols. Philadelphia, 1951.

THE GREAT AWAKENING

15 BELDEN, Albert D. *George Whitefield, the Awakener: A Modern Study of the Evangelical Revival.* New York, 1953.

16 BRINK, Frederick W. "Gilbert Tennent, Dynamic Preacher." *J Presby Hist Soc,* XXXII (1954), 91-109.

17 BRYNESTAD, Lawrence E. "The Great Awakening in the New England and Middle Colonies." *J Presby Hist Soc,* XIV (1930), 80-91, 104-141.

1 FRELINGHUYSEN, Peter H. B., Jr. *Theodorus Jacobus Frelinghuysen.* Princeton, 1938.

2 GAUSTAD, Edwin S. *The Great Awakening in New England.* New York, 1957.

3 GEWEHR, Wesley M. *The Great Awakening in Virginia, 1740-1790.* Durham, N.C., 1930.

4 GOODWIN, Gerald. "The Anglican Reaction to the Great Awakening." *Hist Mag P E Ch,* XXXV (1966), 343-371.

5 HARDY, Edwin N. *George Whitefield, The Matchless Soul Winner.* New York, 1938.

6 HAROUTUNIAN, Joseph. *Piety Versus Moralism: The Passing of the New England Theology.* New York, 1932.

7 HENRY, Stuart C. *George Whitefield (1714-1770): Wayfaring Witness.* New York, 1957.

8 MAXSON, Charles II. *The Great Awakening in the Middle Colonies.* Chicago, 1920.

9 MILLER, John C. "Religion, Finance, and Democracy in Massachusetts." *N Eng Q,* VI (1933), 29-58.

10 MILLER, Perry, *Jonathan Edwards.* See **25.4.**

11 MILLER, Perry. "Jonathan Edwards and the Great Awakening." In *America in Crisis.* Ed. Daniel Aaron. New York, 1952.

12 MILLER, Perry. "Jonathan Edwards' Sociology of the Great Awakening." *N Eng Q,* XXI (1948), 50-77.

13 MITCHELL, Mary H. *The Great Awakening and Other Revivals in the Religious Life of Connecticut.* New Haven, 1934.

14 MORGAN, David T. "The Great Awakening in North Carolina. 1740-1775: The Baptist Phase." *N C Hist Rev.* XLV (1968), 264-283.

15 PARKES, Henry B. "New England in the Seventeen-Thirties." *N Eng Q,* III (1930), 397-419.

16 TOLLES, Frederick B. "Quietism Versus Enthusiasm: The Philadelphia Quakers and the Great Awakening." *Pa Mag Hist,* LXIX (1945), 26-49.

17 WHITE, Eugene E. "Decline of the Great Awakening in New England: 1741 to 1746" *N Eng Q,* XXIV (1951), 35-52.

REVIVALISM AND SEPARATISM

18 BUMSTED, J. M. "Revivalism and Separatism in New England: The First Society of Norwich, Connecticut, as a Case Study." *Wm Mar Q,* 3rd ser., XXIV (1967), 588-612.

19 GOEN, C. C. *Revivalism and Separatism in New England, 1740-1800: Strict Congregationalists and Separate Baptists in the Great Awakening.* New Haven, 1962.

20 MC LOUGHLIN, William G. "The First Calvinistic Baptist Association in New England, 1754-1767," *Ch Hist,* XXVI (1967), 410-418.

21 MC LOUGHLIN, William G. *Isaac Backus and the American Pietistic Tradition.* Boston, 1967.†

RATIONAL RELIGION

Arminianism and Unitarianism

1 AKERS, Charles W. *Called Unto Liberty: A Life of Jonathan Mayhew, 1720-1766.* Cambridge, Mass., 1964.

2 WRIGHT, Conrad, *The Beginnings of Unitarianism in America.* Boston, 1955†

Deism

3 ALDRIDGE, Alfred Owen. *Benjamin Franklin and Nature's God.* Durham, N.C., 1967.

4 CHRISTIANSEN, Merton A. "Franklin on the Hemphill Trial: Deism versus Presbyterian Orthodoxy." *Wm Mar Q,* 3rd ser., X (1953), 422-440.

5 MORAIS, Herbert M. *Deism in Eighteenth Century America.* New York, 1934.

CHURCH AND STATE

6 GREENE, Evarts B. *Religion and the State, The Making and Testing of an American Tradition.* New York, 1941.†

7 KLEIN, Milton M. "Church, State, and Education: Testing the Issue in Colonial New York." *N Y Hist,* XLV (1964), 291-303.

8 MEYER, Jacob C. *Church and State in Massachusetts from 1740 to 1833, a Chapter in the History of Individual Freedom.* Cleveland, 1930.

9 MILLER, Perry. "The Contribution of the Protestant Churches to Religious Liberty in Colonial America." *Ch Hist,* IV (1935), 57-66.

10 O'CONNOR, Thomas F. "Religious Toleration in New York, 1664-1700." *N Y Hist,* XVII (1936), 391-410.

11 PILCHER, George W. "Samuel Davies and Religious Toleration in Virginia." *Historian,* XXVIII (1965), 48-71.

12 PRATT, John Webb. *Religion, Politics, and Diversity, The Church-State Theme in New York History.* Ithaca, 1967.

13 REED, Susan M. *Church and State in Massachusetts, 1691-1740.* Urbana, Ill., 1914.

14 STOKES, Anson P. *Church and State in the United States.* 3 vols. New York, 1950.

15 STRICKLAND, Reba C. *Religion and the State in Georgia in the Eighteenth Century.* New York, 1939.

16 TUCKER, Louis L. "The Church of England and Religious Liberty at Pre-Revolutionary Yale." *Wm Mar Q,* 3rd ser., XVII (1960), 314-328.

17 WEEKS, Stephen B. *The Religious Development in the Province of North Carolina.* Baltimore, 1892.

18 WERLINE, Albert W. *Problems of Church and State in Maryland during the Seventeenth and Eighteenth Centuries.* South Lancaster, Mass., 1948.

NOTES

INDEX

INDEX

INDEX

INDEX

INDEX

INDEX

INDEX

INDEX

INDEX